food
cafes, markets & eateries

RETAIL SPACES

food cafes, markets & eateries

Judy Shepard

and the editors of *Retail Design International*

RSD Publishing, Inc. New York, NY

cafés & eateries

40 Carrots

Bloomingdale's, New York

MANCINI • DUFFY
New York

40 Carrots began life in 1975 as a 12-stool counter restaurant located in Bloomingdale's department store — one of the first major stores of its kind to open an eatery. Since then the "famous and famously crowded" restaurant has gone through a number of expansions as its popularity has increased. Most recently it has moved to an 8,000 square foot space on the seventh floor of Bloomingdale's flagship on Lexington Avenue, doubling its previous seating capacity in the process.

The new space — designed by Mancini Duffy — is bright and contemporary and, in contrast to the black-and-white color palette of Bloomingdale's, alive with color. The most striking design element — perhaps first noticed and most remembered by patrons — are the free-standing columns wrapped in a custom-designed striped wall covering. These colorful stripes have become a signature of the restaurant with the pattern further translated into printed collateral and placemats —offsetting the classic white Villeroy & Boch china and modern flatware.

Patterned wall plaster and sleek blinds add a play of texture to the space.

Edward Calabrese, Senior Associate at Mancini Duffy states, *"Our design program took as its basis vivid, garden-inspired colors and striking oversize graphics offset by a crisp white backdrop. Strong accents such as backlit banquette seating in vibrant orange, a grass-green acrylic mock chair rail, and glazed butterscotch wall tiles in the service area are contrasted with white architectural details such as textural plaster walls, ceiling soffits, and sleek decorative blinds."*

The designers' garden aesthetic is also evidenced in their extensive use of natural materials, such as chairs and seating-area flooring made of reconstituted bamboo and sand-colored porcelain tiles in service and heavy traffic areas. Everywhere one looks in the open and light-filled space there are accents of orange and green amidst notes of neutral tones.

Since 40 Carrots has long been famous for its yogurt, which drives a significant amount of take-out business, the designers focused much of their planning on streamlining the traffic flow and ease of transactions in the busy space. Communications and signage incorporate digital menu boards and flat-screen TV monitors to further enhance the customer experience and smooth operations in this vibrant, modern restaurant.

40 Carrots' new space seats 100 people and, thanks to efficient design, can accommodate a large and rushed lunch crowd. Chairs and seating-area flooring are made from reconstituted bamboo.

DESIGN: **MANCINI • DUFFY,** New York, NY
SENIOR VP STORE PLANNING AND DESIGN, BLOOMINGDALE'S: **Jack Hruska**
LIGHTING CONSULTANT: **Doug Russell, Lighting Workshop,** Brooklyn, NY
PHOTOGRAPHY: **Mancini Duffy**

The restaurant supports a thriving take-out business thanks to its famous yogurt.

Addict Juice Bar

Bengaluru, Karnataka, India

Future Research Design Company
Bangalore, India

The space keeps consumers visually engaged and encourages social interaction.

Juice bars, like coffee shops, are as much about selling the experience as about selling the juice itself. Therefore, when Future Research Design Company (FRDC) was concepting a new signature store for Addict Juice Bar the designers had to be sure that the ambience of the store reflect the defining attributes of the brand — energy, vibrancy, and social awareness. The store had to be fresh and dynamic and stand out from the competition while signaling to all that Addict was a leader in market trends.

An extensive series of market surveys and trend reports led the design team to conclude that the juice bar needed to communicate an atmosphere of relaxation, freshness and youthfulness. Target customers are health conscious individuals of all sorts: young professionals, fitness addicted teenagers and mothers with children. The shop had to not only be a place to consume healthy juices, but also a place to socialize in a relaxed and informal atmosphere,

without the worry of spending too much.

Sanjay Agarwal, Founder and Director of FRDC, states, *"There was an effort made to not replicate the 'loud' and 'overdone' ambience found in various coffee shops these days. Customers have no option but to visit these places and they have developed a 'been there' attitude toward them. Moreover existing coffee shops tend to project a more 'business like' ambience in order to appeal to that class of people. The idea for Addict was to have a differentiated environment suited to youth and all 'health' conscious people, and at the same time not be too over powering."*

The first challenge was the trapezoidal and irregular shape of the space. To visually reshape the space and provide fluidity, long flowing arcs were introduced both on the ceiling and, via a vinyl pattern, on the floor. The central counter/bar follows these arcs with an arc of its own.

The visual language of the space is all about color

The main counter follows the arc of the space with an inviting arc of its own. On the ceiling above the counter a series of red shot glasses serve as lighting fixtures and become a focal point and a topic of conversation for customers.

ABOVE: As customers enter they are carried into the space by the arcs on the floor and ceiling and are able to move effortlessly along the curves . BELOW LEFT: The organic shape of the counter is paired with organic greenery. BELOW RIGHT: Customized furniture and recreational corners with magazines and games give the café a social networking ambience.

RIGHT: Points of bright colors on the menu boards contrast with the neutral tones of the walls and counter. BELOW RIGHT: Signage containing information about the products and the brand are positioned near the counter.

DESIGN: **Future Research Design Company Pvt Ltd,** Bangalore, India

CLIENT: **Elements Food and Beverage Co.**

FIXTURES AND FURNITURE: **Essentially Metals,** Bangalore

LIGHTING: **Philips and Pasolite**

PHOTOGRAPHY: **Mr. Durga,** Bangalore

HVAC: **Toshiba and Carrier**

STORE SIZE: **190 m2** (2,045 Sq. ft.)

and energy. Red, orange, green and yellow mosaic tiles enliven the back wall of the service counter, while the menu boards above are also splashed with color. Bright graphics depicting adventure sports dot the space and include the Addict tagline, "get high on life." The clean white walls and neutral tones of the floor, seating and furniture allow the points of bright color to pop.

Seating for twos and fours is provided for customers who desire privacy, while seating arrangements near the corners cater to those who wish to interact with other customers, play games or browse through a magazine. High stools allow yet others customers to survey the scene. To further encourage customers to linger, customized furniture incorporates games and a book rack provides books on yoga and other health-related topics.

Agarwal sums up the space, *"The name of the Brand itself, Addict, conjures up all that is long lasting, a licensed addiction to all good things. Fun and madness have been designed to create a cool and happening space where one can experience all that is healthy and happy, like the product itself."*

Au Bon Pain
Boston

Interbrand Design Forum
Dayton, Ohio

One of the first remodeled Au Bon Pain locations opened in Boston. The company expects to open many more locations incorporating Interbrand Design Forum's new design.

ABOVE AND OPPOSITE BOTTOM: The dining area offers a variety of seating options including banquettes, bar-height seating and "two top" tables that can be pushed together for added flexibility. Although having a similar seat count to previous Au Bon Pain locations, the new dining area is more well-defined. Warm woods are paired with fabrics in "food-centric" colors to add comfort and color to the space.

Au Bon Pain, a bakery/café chain with more than 300 locations in the U.S. and internationally, recently partnered with Interbrand Design Forum to create an updated and more engaging "marketplace" design for future locations. The focus was on giving the store more personality, distinction and improving the ease of shopping.

Market research and careful analysis of the existing Au Bon Pain experience identified "pain points" and told the team at Interbrand Design Forum that there was significant opportunity for the brand to differentiate itself in the fast-casual category.

"The biggest issue that we needed to address was that Au Bon Pain did not have a personality or tone of voice. When people thought of Au Bon Pain, they thought of yellow bakery," says Tom Kowalski, VP of Design, Interbrand Design Forum. *"The new concept gives the brand credit for the things that is does really well. We've created destinations for core competencies and we've made it easier for customers to* navigate the experience, inviting them to buy more."

The "yellow bakery" is still very much in evidence — yellow is still the brand's signature color — but it's now refreshed with notes of green and accents of berry and chocolate, and part of a more comprehensive and vibrant visual style.

Greatly improved upon with the new design are ease of circulation and product communication. Clearly defined and labeled zones allow customers to quickly and easily assemble their selections. The bakery zone, for instance, with its tempting croissants, cookies and other baked goods, is adjacent to the coffee "island," making breakfast a snap. The soup zone utilizes a custom designed, double-decker fixture that allows ten varieties of soup to be available below and a wide assortment of bread above. The same fixture includes a case for half sandwiches, allowing for a quick lunch assembly.

The Café Creations zone anchors the back of the space, and with the new, efficient wireless-device

LEFT: The soup zone presents all the makings for a light lunch close at hand, thanks to a custom-designed, two-tiered fixture. BOTTOM LEFT: The large selection of fresh salad ingredients can be seen at a glance.

DESIGN: **Interbrand Design Forum,** Dayton, OH

CERAMIC TILE (FLOOR & WALL): **Daltile,** Dallas, TX

PAINT FINISHES: **Benjamin Moore,** Montvale, NJ

PLASTIC LAMINATES: **Lamin-Art,** Schaumburg, IL; **Formica,** Cincinnati, OH; **Liri America Corp.,** Fairfield, NJ

FABRIC FINISHES: **ArcCom Fabrics, Inc.,** Orangeburg, NY

METAL FINISHES: **Chemetal,** East Hampton, MA

SIGNAGE & GRAPHICS: **View Point Sign,** Marlborough, MA; **Visual Graphic Systems,** Carlstadt, NJ

FIXTURES: **Structural Concepts ,** Muskegon, MI; **Mr. O's Custom Millwork & Store Fixtures,** North Canton, OH

FURNITURE: **Beaufurn,** Winston-Salem NC

PHOTOGRAPHER: **Mark La Rosa, Mark La Rosa Photography,** Brooklyn, NY

STORE SIZE: **244.5 m2** (2,632 sq. ft.)

The Bakery and Cafe Creations areas are both clearly communicated and easy to shop.

ordering system enables customers to quickly order customized sandwiches and salads. Communication via the overhead menu board clearly organizes the available options, reducing stress — especially for first-time customers — and ordering time for all. For those in an extreme rush there are already-prepared sandwiches and side items available close by.

The various zones are identified with contemporary signage that combines large, slightly jumbled san-serif text labels with brand messages in script. Artwork on the dining room walls incorporates the same fonts on large, framed, text-based signage and hanging glass dividing panels.

As customers enter the cafe they are guided

through the upfront dining area to the food selections in the back, by the gentle curve of the floor's tile pattern and overhead soffits. Texture and color punctuate the environment and a balance of modern and traditional materials project a contemporary yet authentic atmosphere. The new design is bright, welcoming and energized.

"We're taking the customer experience to the next level," says Sue Morelli, Chief Executive Officer for Au Bon Pain. "The response we've been getting to our new prototype has validated our decision to accelerate our growth, including going to new markets nationally."

Ben & Jerry's

Burlington, Vermont

Tesser, Inc.

San Francisco

Ben & Jerry's recently tapped Tesser, Inc. to redesign the company's global network of 600 scoop shops. Although widely known for the ice cream it sells by the pint at supermarkets, Ben & Jerry's, founded by Ben Cohen and Jerry Greenfield 30 years ago, decided it was time to revamp its, mostly franchised, scoop shops to bring the design in line with the brand's super-premium products and appeal to a younger, more professional audience.

Tre Musco, Tesser's CEO and Chief Creative Officer, explains *"Some of the challenges arose from the disconnect between what the brand stands for, its DNA, and the look and feel of the scoop shops, particularly in relation to its designated target demographic. We knew that this is a super premium product, which was targeting mostly to young adults. It's a hip brand with roots in social responsibility and activism, and an anti-corporate vibe, but the stores were mostly cartoony and kid-like in look and feel, not conveying any of the brand's attributes or equities."*

The new global store design returns to the roots of the brand and remains true to Ben & Jerry's leadership on environmental issues. Tesser sourced re-used and en-

vironmentally friendly materials throughout the store and created a uniquely premium environment that stands apart from the competition.

The new façade, with its galvanized metal, natural wood and stone, evokes the company's roots and its commitment to its quality diary products and the family farm. Inside, Ben & Jerry's ever-present Holstein cows

The exterior sign features a new tie-dye ampersand and the memorable, but until now, under-leveraged tag line "Peace, Love and Ice Cream."

RIGHT: The menu board construction avoids environmentally harmful materials and promotes the brands premium, non-ice cream products expanding the brand experience to more than just a scoop of ice cream. **BELOW:** The funky "Flavor Curtain" was Inspired by hippie-pad bead curtains and features actual pint-carton lids.

DESIGN: **Tesser, Inc.,**
San Francisco, CA

PHOTOGRAPHY: **Jim Westphalen**
www.jimwestphalen.com

also received some remodeling. Now cut out of plywood and mounted on an also revamped mural, the cows have a richer dimensional effect.

Mounted on the back wall and inspired by the founders' original delivery van is what appears to be the front end of a vintage VW van. It doubles as a frame, disguising a pair of monitors that loop videos showing the company's products and social causes.

A redesigned and engineered menu board highlights the offerings, while putting emphasis on the premium, high-margin treats such as smoothies and blended drinks. *"At first glance,"* says Musco, *"the new menu board looks like something that one of Ben and Jerry's carpenter buddies might have made for*

them — a distinct shift from their previous backlit boards. In fact, it's an industry-first system featuring cleverly engineered printed plywood panels mounted on a hook-and-pole system that makes item change-outs fast and easy."

Tesser also rethought the seating area to encourage the sort of gatherings favored by young adults. Installed were contemporary café tables, oak chairs and a couch that mirrors the rolling Vermont hills of the cow mural.

Musco concludes, *"With a variety of remodeled stores open in the U.S. and abroad the votes are in — sales are up and customers are digging the Peace and Love!"*

Body Café
Monroe, Louisiana

Commercial Design Interiors, LLC
Baton Rouge, Louisiana

Renderings of the service line and dining area.

"Fuel for the Body" is the catchphrase for this innovative new space that's part café, part retailer. Body Café strives to promote health and wellness in a community environment, serving freshly-ground coffee, vitamin-boosting smoothies and crepes made with all-natural ingredients. Also on offer are a wide array of vitamins and supplements.

The client, a young entrepreneur, hired Commercial Design Interiors, LLC of Baton Rouge, Louisiana to develop an intuitive, energetic and inviting design that would combine the social scene of a coffee shop,

the niche market of a health-conscious café and the wellness products of a supplement store.

Matthew Edmonds of Commercial Design Interiors explains, *"The design had to incorporate the preconceived logo and marketing with materials and finishes that reinforced the heath conscious concept and the client's catchphrase "fuel for the body" into a fully branded space."*

The resulting design directly references the imagery resembling a "fuel gauge" that exists in the marketing. The curvature of the bar millwork, wall

The orange "indicator" lighting element references the "fuel gauge" graphics found in the marketing and ties into the brands "fuel for the body" marketing. The linear arrangement of the orange chairs mimics the ceiling element and leads the eye to the focal retail wall at the back of the space.

The dining area incorporates booth seating and reconfigurable tables that allow diners to change the space. "Fuel gauge" graphics decorate the wall.

The greens and oranges of the design appear in signage and labels. Reconfigurable retail fixtures provide flexibility for various-sized products while frames allow signage to be changed. The industrial metallic finish reinforces the concept of strength.

graphics and the orange "indicator" ceiling elements all abstractly reconstruct a "gauge" and reinforce the concept of "Fuel for the Body."

Effective space planning encourages the flow of customers down the service line and through the retail area in the rear of the space before reaching the dining area. Once there, customers are able to reconfigure the "two-top" tables as needed for group interaction.

A color palette of bold hues of green and orange energize the space while a materials list that includes durable "raw" industrial materials and concrete emphasizes the branding concept of vitality, power and strength.

The designers also had to be mindful of the budget while meeting the client needs. Edmonds explains, "*We needed to minimize the use of custom millwork while sourcing readily available and reconfigurable retail fixtures to ensure the cost effectiveness of the design while allowing it to be easily reproduced for future franchise locations.*"

DESIGN: **Commercial Design Interiors, LLC,** Baton Rouge, LA

DESIGNERS: **Matthew Edmonds, Tracy Burns, Stephen Knight**

GENERAL CONTRACTOR: **Vicari Construction (Mike Vicari, Pete Vicari, PJ Vicari, Barbara Vicari)**

RETAIL MANAGEMENT CONSULTANT: **Christian Galvin**

LIGHTING: **Commercial Design Interiors, LLC,** Baton Rouge, LA

MARKETING GRAPHICS: **Matt Wang, Good Work Marketing**

PHOTOGRAPHY: **Matthew Edmonds**

STORE SIZE: **250 m2** (2,700 sq. ft.)

The curvature of the service line and condiment bar references the "fuel gauge" marketing while leading the customer to the retail area.

Café Mixup

Centro Comercial Plaza Satélite / Palmas, Mexico

Plus Construction Group

Tecamachalco, Mexico

TOP AND ABOVE: The Satélite location was the third Café completed and it's in one of Mexico's largest Mixup stores.

Mixup, Mexico's premier music store chain, recently asked Plus Construction Group to design Café Mixup, a new in-store concept for the music, books, movies and electronics retailer. Mixup's vision was to offer customers a youthful and dynamic environment set apart from the main retail space, in which they could enjoy a cup of coffee while listening to music or browsing through a book — a place to linger and relax.

Shown here are two locations, Café Mixup Satélite, in the shopping center Centro Comercial Plaza Satélite (shown on these two pages), and Café Mixup Palmas, a vendor shop in Palmas (shown on the following two pages). The first Café Mixup in Génova, the prototype, is the only one located in a space adjoining the music store.

The cafés include a service bar for hot and cold beverages, desserts, sandwiches, seating and display areas for Mixup's main products, as well as accessories such as mugs and thermos and even coffee beans.

The main challenge says designer Carlos

TOP AND ABOVE: Located in the back of the store, the Satélite Café is the largest of the three Café Mixups and is adjacent to a book-selling area.

Carreño Cano was, *"finding an identity for the cafés in relation to Mixup, and the search for harmony between the two concepts."*

The main service bars have elegant Baltic brown granite counter tops and metallic decorative elements of aluminum. The bars curve dynamically as does an overhead floating marquee from which the light fixtures are suspended. Orange finishes on the bar add a youthful vigor to the space and helps to differentiate the cafés from the surrounding retailing shops with their grays and blues. The lighting is designed to accentuate the finishes and modern shapes.

The tables have granite tops and stainless steel bases and are surrounded by contemporary white chairs. A wide selection of books are close by and customers are encouraged to gear-down to a peaceful Café Mixup pace.

Café Mixup at the Palmas Mixup, one of the retailers most successful stores. This Café was a challenge due to its location right inside the store entrance. The designers needed to transition shapes and colors from the café to the store in a manner that would connect the spaces.

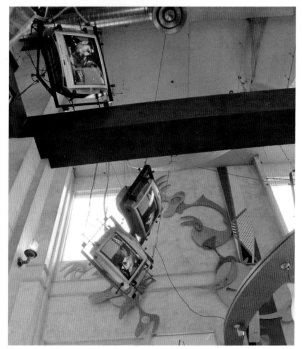

DESIGN: **Plus Construction Group,** Tecamachalco, Mexico

DESIGN/ARCHITECTURE: **Carlos Carreño Cano**

PROJECT MANAGER: **Carlos Carreño Cano**

DIRECTOR OF DESIGN PRODUCTION: **Arturo Cole**

PRINCIPALS IN CHARGE: **Antonio Jimenez / Eduardo Sosa**

BUILDING CONTRACTOR: **Plus Construction Group**

FIXTURES/LIGHTING: **Plus Construction Group**

PHOTOGRAPHY: **Courtesy of the designers**

STORE SIZES: **Satélite, 160 m2** (1,722 sq. ft.);
Palmas, 42 m2 (452 sq. ft.)

Seen from overhead Cafe Mixup at Palmas is clearly a café within an electronic- and entertainment-loving environment. Listening stations were designed to allow customers the experience of enjoying music and a cup of delicious coffee at the same time.

Cafesano

South Lakes Shopping Center, Reston, Virginia

Design Republica
Washington, D.C.

Cafesano is a restaurant in Reston, Virginia, dedicated to the idea that "great taste" and "good for you" can describe the same dining experience. The food and flavors of Italy, Greece and the Mediterranean — considered by many to be the world's healthiest — fill the menu, including fresh vegetables, select meats and diary products, savory Mediterranean herbs and spices, and the exclusive use of olive oil.

Design Republica was brought onboard to create a casual, warm and inviting space that would transport guests to a Mediterranean oasis, far away from their hectic daily schedules. Available would be healthy options for sit-down dining as well as

DESIGN: **Design Republica, Inc.,** Washington, D.C.

PROJECT TEAM: **Francisco A. Beltran, AIA; Jeanne M. Jarvaise; Enoc Joel Montilla**

STORE SIZE: **275 m2 (2,964 sq. ft.)**

PHOTOGRAPHY: **Charma Le Edmonds, Shelter Studios**

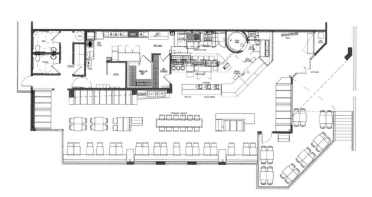

Dry stacked stone was used on feature walls and low voltage lighting illuminates the food display cases.

facilities for take-out service. Additionally, the clients wanted Cafesano to transform into a more upscale environment in the evenings, offering the residents of Reston an elegant dining option without having to drive into Washington.

The location the clients selected for Cafesano was nestled between a small shopping center and the picturesque South Lake. The restaurant that had previously occupied the space had not taken advantage of the beautiful lake views, having instead covered the windows with blinds and heavy drapes. There was also a drop ceiling that was found to conceal a large loft space. Because of the dark and uninviting space, and an ill-designed kitchen that no longer met building code requirement, the decision was made to gut the space and start over.

Francisco Beltran, AIA, Principal at Design Republica explains, *"We exposed the previously hidden ceiling areas to maximize the interior heights. The walls and ceilings were painted white in order to allow the light to travel deep into the restaurant. Dry stacked stone was used to accent feature walls and to convey the natural colors and textures found on the Greek islands. The concrete floors were stained and sealed to allow the natural imperfections in the concrete to come through and to add yet another layer of texture. We introduced low voltage lighting to illuminate the food display cases and we finished the pizza oven with a custom mosaic glass tile."*

Centered in the space is a 14-foot granite-top communal table that provides a natural barrier between the order-placing counter and the dining area, as well as offering an alternate, communal, dining experience for customers. Decorative, over-sized pendant fixtures are centered over the table and small, hand-blown lighting accents line the perimeter of the dining area with a vibrant blue glow.

In the evening, the elegant, faux leather banquettes are offset against the walnut-stained concrete floor and the stone accent walls to create a warm, yet hip environment. Since opening, Cafesano has met with rave reviews and become a popular neighborhood destination.

ABOVE: The natural light flooding the space and the additional ceiling height gained by exposing a loft space give Cafesano an open and inviting atmosphere. BELOW: One of the designers' models and their concept board.

Carrefour Laval Food Court

Laval, Quebec

GHA design studios

Ceiling heights in the vast new space range from 20 feet to over 37 feet in the central skylight area.

Following an award-winning expansion in 2003 Carrefour Laval, a shopping center in Quebec, needed to consolidate two satellite food courts into one new location while upgrading the image. GHA design studios was called upon to perform the transformation. *"The goal was to lift an often uneventful food court experience to one that matches the level of high style of the previous general mall expansion/renovation, and one that rivals contemporary food courts internationally from both aesthetic and tenancy points of views,"* states Debbie Kalisky, Director of Retail Development.

The result is the Dining Terrace, an oasis of urban sophistication and style — the not-a-food-court food-court — and now one of the largest shopping center food destinations in Canada with seating for 1050 patrons. The new space integrates all the outlets of the former two courts, including local restaurateurs, into one unprecedented food experience.

Kalisky explains, *"Challenges ranged from having restaurateurs adjust their operations to a fast food format to seasoned fast food operators having to depart from their existing formulas and embrace the new vision of the Dining Terrace. For example, menu boards had to conform to modern font styles and clean graphic presentation. A design review committee evaluated each tenant submission and made detailed recommendations and alternative design proposals to ensure the high standards of the Design Criteria were being met."*

The use of prominent free-standing island units, each with its own seating area, allowed tenants to showcase bold designs and maximize their exposure while adhering to the overall aesthetic objective. A cohesive look among the perimeter tenants was achieved by presenting their diverse logos on otherwise identical signage.

One of the upscale niceties, the use of real dishware and cutlery, brought with it the nitty-gritty problem of how to handle the dishwashing load of 14,000 dishes per hour. The industrial equipment necessary for the job had to be located at a distance to avoid becoming a sound and visual nuisance, yet within easy "cartable" distance from the dining area.

TOP: A layered approach to the ceiling planes provides an architecturally varied experience while establishing a neutral backdrop for the outstanding tenant designs. ABOVE LEFT: One of the dangers associated with a large hall with generous seating capacity is the potential "cafeteria effect." This was prevented by providing a wide variety of seating zones, incorporating several seating arrangements and styles. ABOVE RIGHT: One of the cornerstones of the new design was the use of prominent island units.

DESIGN: **GHA design studios**
FOOD COURT SIZE: **19,000 sq. ft.**
LIGHTING CONSULTANT: **Philip Gabriel,** Ottawa, ON
GENERAL CONTRACTOR: **C.A.L.,** St. Laurent, QC
MILLWORK/FURNITURE: **Ébénisterie St. Patrick,** Laval, QC
PLUMBING: **Mechanitech,** Montréal, QC

TILES: **Stone Tile,** Toronto/**Ciot,** Montréal
TILE INSTALLATION: **National Ceramic and Granite Ltd.,** St. Laurent, QC
GLASS: **Euroverre, Laval**
SIGNAGE: **Techno Plus Montreal**
PHOTOGRAPHER: **Yves Lefebvre,** Montréal

DUCE

Fort Worth, Texas

The Michael Malone Studio at WKMC Architects
Dallas, Texas

DUCE is the second restaurant concept developed by noted chef and restaurateur Tom Love, owner of Lonesome Dove, also in Forth Worth. For DUCE Love wanted a less formal concept based on lighter Mediterranean style fare and specialty drinks. The menu Love developed emphasizes multiple, smaller courses, conducive to a longer dining experience.

The Michael Malone Studio at WKMC Architects was asked to design a space that was fresh, innovative and sophisticated, but still comfortable and casual. Michael Malone explains, *"With the increasing recognition of Lonesome Dove as one of the nation's most innovative restaurants, Tim and his wife Emilie wanted this restaurant to reflect their success and maturity as business people and set a new direction for Tim's exploration and reinterpretation of a whole new type of cuisine. DUCE was to*

be a vehicle for that activity, as Lonesome Dove had been for Southwestern cuisine. Tim described it as place people would eat every week, if not more as opposed to Lonesome Dove which was a more special meal or business dinner environment."

The designers broke up the seating into multiple, smaller spaces that incorporate a variety of seating configurations, including banquets in alcoves, conventional two and four top tables and several shared seating areas with low tables. Also included in the design, and considered an integral part of the DUCE experience, is an outdoor seating area. In deference to the variable Texas climate this area is covered with an elaborate trellis structure that incorporates infrared heaters for chilly evenings. A central feature of the outdoor area — one that emphasizes relief from the often hot Texas

ABOVE: The curving interior bar is the central gathering space and heart of DUCE. The base alternates douglas fir bands with strips of stainless steel and the top is cast-in-place concrete finished to match the floors. The douglas fir screen behind the bar is actually in front of a glass window that looks into the kitchen. A curving soffit overhead reinforces the shape of the bar. OPPOSITE: The facade incorporates the standard shopping center tower element and finishes with the signature DUCE wood and glass storefront.

ABOVE LEFT: Among the variety of seating types are these two, 12-person booths. Finished in douglas fir and upholstered in cream leather, they are a comfortable place for large groups. The walls above and the banquet itself are paneled in strips of douglas fir and stainless steel. Above the booths and extending from the adjacent bar, is the curving wine storage closets, accessible from a rolling ladder. The collage was made by the architect as a gift to the Loves on the opening of the restaurant. ABOVE RIGHT: A sheltered dining alcove — set off from the larger dining area with a lower ceiling and more intimate scale — provides a private place for diners to enjoy a quiet conversation.

weather — is a curving fountain wall with mosaic tile in a pattern designed by the architects.

Two large, full-service bars, one inside, one out, and two fireplaces, also interior and exterior, are vital to the relaxed atmosphere of DUCE. Seating around the fireplaces is casual and relaxed and, as with the bars, are intended as informal meeting places.

Natural cherry and douglas fir finishes are used throughout DUCE, in wall panels, tables, banquets and millwork. Stainless steel accents are incorporated into the bar, table tops and various custom metal items fabricated for the space. The floors are stained concrete and a curved, climate-controlled wine storage unit is placed above the bar, accessible from a rolling ladder.

As with most projects, the design had to be realized within a stringent budget, including the creation of a full-service gourmet-style commercial kitchen, two new sets of rest rooms for interior and exterior use and the building of the outdoor dining area from scratch.

"To meet the challenges of the project," says Malone, "the design was pared down to the essentials and each element was studied to determine how best to execute it as economically as possible. Further, it was determined which areas would be developed in the most detailed and expensive manner to assure the maximum impact. It was decided that the two bars, the fountain wall and the fireplaces with their associated seating would get the most attention and budget resources. The rest of the finish out was accomplished as economically as possible, with the floors being sealed and stained concrete, the walls painted gypsum board (except for areas that received paneling accents) and the ceilings left open and painted a dark color to camouflage the ductwork."

ABOVE: The interior dining room is loosely organized around three elements: the curving bar; traditional table seating; and an enclosed seating alcove. Ceiling forms define various focal points in the restaurant and stand out against the darkened ceiling structure. BELOW: This seating area in front of the interior fireplace is enclosed in a douglas fir surround with cream leather upholstery. Low tables and stools allow the area to be organized informally for as many groups and individuals as can fit comfortably.. Food can be served here, but the main emphasis is on cocktails and conversation.

The outdoor seating area, sheltered under its trellis, includes a full bar to ensure patrons have the same beverage options as those indoors. The variable Texas weather is countered with both a fireplace for chilly evenings and a fountain for hot summer days. The doors to the interior dining room can be opened on nice days to allow the two spaces to flow continuously together, and a stage at one end is perfect for live music.

DESIGN: **The Michael Malone Studio at WKMC Architects,** Dallas, TX
PHOTOGRAPHER: **Steven Vaughan Photography,** Dallas, TX

Giacomo

Berlin

Plajer & Franz Studio
Berlin

When Plajer & Franz was charged with the design of the café Giacomo they first had to examine the meanings and implications of the term "gourmet fast food" — the generating concept behind the café. Instead of thinking of the term as a contradiction in terms, the designers drew on the best of both worlds — gourmet and fast food — to conceptualize the space. The high quality and emotional authenticity of a gourmet shop had to be incorporated into a cafe that would meet the needs of customers with little time to spare.

"In a world where time has become the greatest luxury and where work and leisure time tend to blend more and more, it is essential to provide the customer with fast and proper service. Therefore, it is not inappropriate to sell fast food, because for Giacomo, fast food does not equate to eating quickly, but to being attended to quickly and exclusively," states

Alexander Plajer from Plajer & Franz Studio. The challenge for the designers was to reflect these values in the design of the space in a Wilhelminian-style building on a tree-lined Berlin street.

For inspiration the designers looked across the globe to the appealing and fluid shapes found in

Overhead lighting and spot lights, combined with a light source placed around the circumference of the space where the ceiling and walls meet, create a glowing, floating atmosphere.

Asian architecture, and mixed in references to modernity and its contemporary proportions. *"Light and free flowing shapes appear in Asian residential architecture over a thousand year ago, where communication and the sense of community were the most essential elements,"* says Plajer. *"At Giacomo the individual spaces flow into one another, underscored by the well-directed use of lighting."*

The dark floor and still darker ceiling, combined with the subtle lighting and white walls, create a space that seems to exist slightly out of time with the busy street life outside the door, placing the customer in an elegant, but relaxed, environment.

Finishes and colors, including specific shades of gold, are carefully aligned with Giacomo's corporate design to create a consistent message and a high degree of brand recognition. Modern materials and technology are utilized to fulfill all of the functional aspects of a fast food establishment and guarantee a smooth workflow behind the counter. The result is a setting that meets all the needs of a busy café while conveying quality service and product.

Plajer sums up the firms intent: *"For Plajer & Franz Studio it's always important that our projects do not preach uncompassionate architectural concepts, but always incorporate emotional aspects that speak to the customer. At Giacomo part of the original Wilhelminian-style ceiling has been exposed, playfully integrating this historic reference into the overall design. It's always the hot versus the cold, the rough next to the smooth, that moves people — not the lukewarm."*

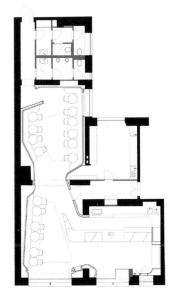

ABOVE RIGHT: Part of the building's original ceiling was left exposed and serves as a backdrop for the modern lighting fixtures.
BELOW: Mirrors are utilized to open up the space and complement the modern aesthetic.

DESIGN: **Plajer & Franz,** Berlin, Germany

SIZE: **140 m2** (1,507 sq. ft.)

PROJECT MANAGEMENT: **Astrid Dressel**

PHOTOGRAPHER: **Ken Schluchtmann, diephotodesigner.de**

Hog Island Oyster Bar

Oxbow Public Market, Napa, California

BALDAUF CATTON VON ECKARTSBERG Architects

San Francisco

Hog Island Oyster Bar is an anchor tenant in the Oxbow Public Market in Napa, the heart of California's wine country, and follows on the success of the company's location in San Francisco's Ferry Building Marketplace. The Oyster Bar serves premium grade oysters farmed by the Hog Island Oyster Company in Tomales Bay, an inlet of the Pacific Ocean 50 miles north of San Francisco. The company was founded in 1983 by three marine biologists and today prides itself on its sustainable farming practices.

The market location means that the new Hog Island Oyster Bar is surrounded with a bustling artisan food community as well as the rich, unique character of Napa Valley. In response to the wine country setting, the designers and architects at BALDAUF CATTON VON ECKARTSBERG Architects, the firm responsible for the bar (and also designers of the market itself), chose a warm and organic materials palette to create a casual dining experience. Warm, cast stone countertops feature sea fossils and reclaimed wood planks line the seating counter face.

The main focus of the space is the large oyster bar itself, which allows patrons front-row views of the oyster-shucking. On prominent display overhead, hangs a vintage, refurbished Hog Island fishing boat previously used on the company's farm in Tomales Bay. Together with a large company sign, the bar and boat form a centerpiece to the bar that's eye-catching and inviting — and can be seen throughout the market building.

Also eye-catching are views of the nearby Napa River. Although the Oxbow Public Market is located in the town of Napa itself, Hog Island Oyster Bar overlooks a bend in the Napa River and views through the floor-to-ceiling windows are spectacular and idyllic, the perfect accompaniment to a fine meal. An exterior patio allows patrons an even closer experience of the surrounding landscape.

ABOVE: The main focus of the space is the large bar where customers can watch oyster-shucking. Overhead hangs a vintage Hog Island fishing boat, previously used for actual operations at the Hog Island Oyster Farm in Tomales Bay. BELOW: The gray cast stone counter tops feature sea fossils, and reclaimed wood planks line the seating counter.

DESIGN: **BALDAUF CATTON VON ECKARTSBERG Architects,** San Francisco, CA
CONTRACTOR: **Terra Nova,** Walnut Creek, CA
PHOTOGRAPHER: **Rien van Rijthoven Architecture Photography**

Hog Island Oyster Bar's location, on the river side of the Oxbow Public Market, allows spectacular water views and the opportunity for patrons to sit on the exterior patio overlooking the Napa River.

La Birreria

New York

TPG Architecture

New York

La Birreria is a rooftop brewery and restaurant located 15 stories above the street on top of New York City's historic Toy Building at 23rd Street and Fifth Avenue. The 4,500 sq. ft. roof deck offers craft beers brewed on the premises and a full rustic-Italian menu as well as wines on tap. Located on the ground floor, and through which patrons of La Birreria must enter, is Eataly, the popular and all-things-Italian market/café. Both establishments are owned by Batali and Bastianich Hospitality Group.

TPG Architecture of New York designed La Birreria to evoke a 1920s industrial brewery with copper-clad brewing vats set against black subway tiling. Custom brass light fixtures lead the eye toward the majestic New York City skyline that surrounds the building. The 22-seat bar is topped with white Carrara marble and the tables are made with salvaged wood. The entire space seats 150 patrons and is equipped with a retractable enclosure to allow year-round operation.

The rooftop location brought with it a series of challenges for the designers. A deck had to be built capable of handling the restaurant, a full-service kitchen, bar and 200 people. A full-scale mock-up, using poles and tarp, had to be built on the roof to ensure that nothing would be seen from the street. A requirement of the Landmarks Committee.

OPPOSITE: Important to an establishment that brews its own craft beers is showing patrons something of the process. La Birreria displays copper-clad vats surrounded by black tiling. ABOVE: A retractable roof allows views of the Manhattan skyline . BELOW: Every element of the design, from the signage to the beer taps, contributes to the 1920s industrial brewery atmosphere.

ABOVE AND BELOW: Customers are taken by elevator to a 14th floor vestibule where they continue via stairs (or an wheelchair lift). The stairs themselves are utilized to "speak" to ascending customers.

DESIGN: **TPG Architecture,** New York, NY
Lisa Eaton, Batali and Bastianich Hospitality Group, New York, NY
KEY PROJECT PERSONNEL: **Alec Zaballero, Vlad Zadneprianski, Diana Revkin**
LIGHTING: **Lighting Workshop,** New York, NY
MEP ENGINEER: **AMA Consulting Engineers,** New York, NY
STRUCTURAL ENGINEER: **Severud Associates,** New York, NY
GENERAL CONTRACTOR: **Structure Tone,** New York, NY
MILLWORK: **Scanga Architectural Woodworking,** Cold Spring, NY
STEELWORK: **USW,** Congers, NY
ARCHITECTURAL METAL AND GLASS: **A-Val,** Mt. Vernon, NY
SIGNAGE: **Artfx,** Bloomfield, CT
PHOTOGRAPHER: **Alec Zaballero, TPG Architecture,** New York, NY

Also a challenge caused by the rooftop location was getting the enormous amount of steel needed hoisted to the roof. Only a few cranes in New York State were capable of the job and a special permit had to be obtained to close the very busy 23rd Street for a day.

The high volume of customers anticipated necessitated the installation of two dedicated elevators. The elevators go to the 14th floor, one down from the roof. Stairs, and a wheelchair lift, take customers the rest of the way. Because of the very small overlap between the two floors there was a play of only inches for the stairs, lift and bathrooms.

Pam Jacobs, Director of Marketing at TPG Architecture sums up the subsequent success, "*La Birreria, like Eataly, is a huge success. The crowds are so thick that a buzzer system has been implemented, like at a theme park, to allow people access to the roof.*"

La Provence
Artisanal French Bakery & Café
Miami

Ruscio Studio
Montréal

La Provence Artisanal French Bakery & Café began producing authentic French delicacies, including bread, croissants and pastries, in 1997 after founding partner David Thau moved to Miami from France. The bakery's original shop was located in the heart of South Beach and baked fresh goods on the premises daily.

Initially catering mainly to a breakfast and lunch crowd, the bakery's popularity grew with locals and tourists alike and soon there were lines to get into the shop forming throughout the day. The bakery had also, by that time, established itself as a supplier to gourmet restaurants and fine hotels. The need to expand and redefine their image was apparent.

Ruscio Studio was hired to guide the bakery through its expansion. The firm, located in bilingual Montréal, offered the cultural diversity and European influence for which La Provence was looking.

With plans to add several locations in the greater Miami area, it became necessary to centralize the baking process off-premises. This in turn, made it vital that the design of the new cafés clearly communicate the two most important defining characteristics of the brand — freshness and authenticity.

Inspiration for these crucial elements was found in the café namesake —the unique color palette and lavender fields of the region of La Provence in the South of France. The incorporation of olive green walls, marble countertops, a random-patterned limestone floor and the lavender field mural were all key elements in rendering the needed authenticity.

Although the completely functional baking kitchen was to be centralized, a conscious decision was made to add warming ovens in each of the new cafés. These ovens are visible to the public and allow customers to see, and *smell,* the fresh baked breads being warmed. The aroma of the warming bread communicates a sense of freshness to anyone entering the shop.

In less than two years, five new locations have opened in the Miami-Dade area. La Provence French Artisan Bakery and Café has received extremely positive feedback from both existing and new clients and is planning to continue with their Miami expansion.

Imported Parisian wicker bistro chairs, tables and dark oak units emphasize the French lifestyle. Chalkboards are used as menu boards, allowing flexibility and encompassing a traditional bakery style.

Since the original café was meant to operate only during daylight hours, and the new locations cater to morning, lunch and evening crowds, the lighting had to be completely redesigned. Perimeter track lighting, hidden above the floating ceiling, accentuates the dark walls and creates a more dramatic mood, especially during the evening hours.

DESIGN: **Ruscio Studio,** Montréal, QC, Canada
PHOTOGRAPHY: **Ruscio Studio**

Marra

Cantù, Italy

Costa Group
Riccò del Golfo, La Spezia, Italy

Simplicity and cleanness of line predominate in the design the Costa Group created for Marra, a multi-functional food retailer in Italy. Included in the two-level space are a bakery, a cafe and areas selling pastry, chocolate and ice cream. After dark, light pours from the large front windows, inviting the hungry passerby in for a treat. The building also houses the food production facility that sup-

plies this shop, as well as other selling points.

Sofas and damask armchairs occupy the open space up front, right inside the windows. An elegant wood floor clearly separates this seating area from the rest of the ceramic-tiled shop. The first, or upper, floor overhangs the first floor, and with a transparent balustrade is clearly visible from the ground level.

THIS PAGE AND OPPOSITE: The ground floor is anchored by a U-shaped counter made of iroko wood with an upper working top of black granite. Lit from the bottom, it allows a wide range of products to be attractively displayed. To right of the counter are the ice cream and café zones. To the left of the counter is the chocolate and sweets zones. A white Corian case, similar to what one may find in a jewelry shop, showcases the chocolate pralines.

THIS PAGE AND OPPOSITE: The upper lever — the refreshment area — has a light and airy atmosphere. The furniture is a mix of iroko tables, small white tables and brown sofas. The counter is light gray glass, again lit from the bottom, and has a working surface of black granite. Black and silver wallpaper covers one wall. The clean, modern lines used throughout the space serve to highlight the quality products and create a relaxed environment to enjoy the goodies.

DESIGN: **Costa Group,** Riccò del Golfo, La Spezia, Italy

DESIGN AND FURNITURE: **Luigi Benvenuti**

PHOTOGRAPHY: **Moreno Carbone**

Pava

Newton Centre, Massachusetts

Bergmeyer Associates, Inc

Boston

Tess Enright and Carlos Pava, the owners of Tess & Carlos, a high-end women's apparel, shoe and accessory boutique, recently wanted to expand their brand by developing a fine dining venue to act in concert with their boutique. With Pava, the restaurant they opened adjacent to Tess & Carlos, they seek to establish and nurture a lavish lifestyle experience for people who appreciate fine food, wine and apparel equally.

Bergmeyer Associates, in collaboration with Enright and Pava, created a bright, clean space, which unites separate buildings and two unlikely functions into one, seamless brand experience. A minimalist décor and views of the couture next door complement the innovative, Mediterranean-inspired menu.

Because the structural columns and the floor levels of the original spaces were not aligned, the design team developed additive and subtractive volumes and planes to conceal oddly-placed beams, ductwork and roof drains. The resulting ceiling structure resembles a contemporary sculpture — consistent with the design and visually interesting. Ramping the floors at a low pitch allows the sidewalk to seamlessly flow into the space, bringing the store into compliance with accessibility regulations and mediating between the existing floor levels.

Through the extensive use of glass and a shared materials palette of raw plaster, polished concrete, stainless steel and ebonized mahogany, an environment is created in which restaurant and boutique act as one.

The open and inviting space incorporates views of both the adjacent boutique and an attractive stretch of Newton Centre outside the large front window. The result is a relaxed, yet sophisticated dining experience.

DESIGN: **Bergmeyer Associates, Inc.,** Boston, MA
PHOTOGRAPHER: **Greg Premru**

PNC Diamond Club

Washington Nationals Ballpark, Washington, D.C.

Perkowitz+Ruth Architects

Reston, Virginia

Just two years after it was completed, the PNC Diamond Club at Washington Nationals Ballpark was deemed out of step with the needs of the current and projected club membership, and in need of renovation. The interior — in stark contrast to the open-air ballpark — was dark and cramped, constricted by columns, trusses and a sloped structural slab that supported seating above the space. The entry consisted of an unadorned storefront window and door that provided no arrival experience for guests. An old-time baseball theme did nothing to lighten the mood.

Perkowitz+Ruth Architects (P+R) was asked to design a contemporary and urban upscale dining and lounge environment. The club's new interior includes a concierge entry, multimedia lounge,

THIS PAGE: The colorful and exciting new facade and entryway enhance the arrival experience for guests, thereby increasing the desirability of membership.
OPPOSITE: Views of the field are now abundant from both the dining room and bar.

cocktail bar and dining room. Using a contemporary design aesthetic, P+R created a high-energy, sleek setting, thereby increasing the desirability of club membership.

The main challenge of the project was its accelerated schedule: all design, permitting and construction had to be completed between the close of Major League Baseball's 2009 season and Opening Day, Spring 2010. Further constricting the schedule was the fact that the PNC Diamond Club had been booked with private events through December, allowing for only a three-month construction schedule.

To achieve the accelerated project schedule, HITT Contracting was brought on board at the beginning of the design process. All consultants worked closely to coordinate the design and construction operations, as well as facilitate the overall budget. *"They [P+R] put out a tremendous effort to get this done in a very short time,"* said Frank Gambino, VP for Facilities for the Washington Nationals. *"Their dedication to the project really stood out in my mind. They worked nights, weekends and right through the holidays."*

The new design creates a strong presence on the concourse level with a new façade and entry that greets quests with a splash of color and excitement. Modern interpretations of classic baseball pennants, custom designed to celebrate DC's baseball heritage, heighten the arrival experience.

Immediately apparent inside the door is the striking architectural dimensions of the walls and their curved radius — all based on baseball field standards including the batter's box, infield base-

lines and pitching mound. The elimination of existing walls, millwork and portions of the ceiling opened up the space, allowing natural light to be the dominant light source for day games. Patrons can now enjoy clubhouse luxuries along with greatly improved field visibility.

The bar is finished with glass mosaics to reflect the natural light and allow it to penetrate further into the space. Custom-designed column covers incorporate the silhouettes of local baseball heroes and are back-lit with LED lights to produce a warm glow and create ambient light. Paying homage to the brick row houses of the surrounding neighborhood is the special craftsman detailing of the brick walls included throughout the space.

The Washington Nationals Ballpark is LEED® Certified-Silver and the PNC Diamond Club project had to meet the sustainability standards of the stadium. Selective demolition of materials for reuse

in the Club, or within other stadium spaces, included lighting, mechanical, electrical and plumbing equipment, as well as kitchen equipment. The existing granite bar top was also repurposed for communal tables.

"The new PNC Diamond Club's design is a celebration of DC's baseball heritage and a nostalgic interpretation of our history," says Joseph Serruya, Associate Principal in charge of P+R's Eastern Region. *"We have created a casual, natty sports venue where baseball enthusiasts can participate as fans, yet relax and be catered to in a clubby atmosphere. The contemporary design offers enhanced ballpark views, maximizes the flow to club seating and creates a high-energy and sleek setting, thus increasing the desirability of the venue to members and potential members."*

ABOVE: Curved leather walls and accents recall baseball gloves. **OPPOSITE:** The excitement of the field is now a prominent feature of the club, and the contemporary design aesthetic created a high-energy sleek setting.

DESIGN: **Perkowitz+Ruth Architects,** Reston, VA

DEVELOPER: **Washington Nationals Stadium, LLC**

LIGHTING DESIGN: **C. M. Kling & Associates, Inc.**

GENERAL CONTRACTOR: **HITT Contracting**

DEVELOPER (KITCHEN): **Levy Restaurants**

STRUCTURAL ENGINEER: **Perkowitz+Ruth Architects**

MEP ENGINEER: **KTA Group, Inc.**

KITCHEN CONSULTANT: **S20 Consultants, Inc.**

AUDIO/VISUAL CONSULTANT: **Shen Milsom Wilke, LLC**

PHOTOGRAPHY: **Kenneth M. Wyner Photography, Inc.**

Table 1280

Woodruff Arts Center, Atlanta

Bergmeyer Associates, Inc
Boston

The Woodruff Arts Center in Atlanta, Georgia, a complex of civic and cultural institutions including the High Museum and the Atlanta Symphony, recently expanded its gallery and performance spaces with a new facility designed by Renzo Piano Building Workshop. Woodruff Arts Center and Restaurant Associates, their food service provider, chose Bergmeyer to design the interior of Table 1280, a restaurant within the center.

The goal of the design was to create a clean, modern and sophisticated multi-functional restaurant catering to museum and symphony attendees, staff and the general public. Themes introduced in Piano's surrounding building had to be continued within Table 1280, giving guests a dining experience consistent with their visit to the arts complex.

A directive from the clients required that a covered walkway connecting the museum and res-

taurant be integrated into the design. This structural element was used by Bergmeyer to organize the various spaces within the restaurant — spaces which are utilized for public and private dining areas, a lounge and bar, kitchen and wine display/storage area. Guests may choose between an Ameri-

View from the main dining room.

can brasserie-inspired meal or the Tapas Lounge while enjoying views of an exterior courtyard and the arts center exhibition space.

High ceilings, floor-to-ceiling windows, clean white walls and the sparing use of color create a sense of transparency and reflection that allows the space to be perceived as an extension of the museum. The contemporary art on display interacts harmoniously with the reflective surfaces, polished wood and custom-designed wine cabinets.

The long host station and the playful "floating" bar were both designed as sculptural elements and are the result of the productive collaboration be-tween designer and fabricator to develop the all-important details of the project. Also "floating" is the massive single-basin sink that passes through the mirrored wall separating the men's and women's rooms and seems to defy gravity — suspended in both rooms.

Indirect and internal lighting add softness and warmth to the space, making Table 1280 a place to linger while enjoying fine food as an art form.

ABOVE AND TOP RIGHT: Seating with a view in the display kitchen. **ABOVE RIGHT:** The main dining room.

The private dining room features artwork from the Woodruff Arts Center's collection.

The tapas bar also includes views of the Arts complex.

The lounge area with the custom-designed wine racks that help define a passageway through the space.

Fixtures such as the wine racks and host station are designed as sculptural elements. A large sink seems to "float," actually passing through a mirrored wall between the men's and women's rooms.

DESIGN: **Bergmeyer Associates, Inc.,** Boston, MA
PHOTOGRAPHER: **Chun Lai Photography**

Virgin Atlantic Clubroom

Logan International Airport, Boston

Bergmeyer Associates, Inc

Boston

Virgin Atlantic Airlines recently commissioned Bergmeyer to design a new, upscale lounge and restaurant for first class passengers within an existing lounge space on the second floor of Terminal E in Boston's Logan International Airport. The designers' intent was to create a space that mirrored the company's unique character while catering to the comfort and ease of the customer — resulting in a first class experience prior to the first class flight.

"Each Virgin Atlantic Clubhouse combines Virgin Atlantic's own style and philosophy with the local *flavor*," states Lewis Muhlfelder, AIA, LEED AP, Principal in Charge of the project from Bergmeyer. *"For the Boston Clubhouse we used patterns and materials inspired by local influence and referencing the historical and modern aspects of Boston. The more prominent materials include wood, stone and stainless steel arranged in patterns reminiscent of shingles and brickwork. The palette is neutral with punches of color accenting the brand and culture of both Virgin Atlantic and Boston."*

One of the requirements from the client was that the space be divided into four distinct areas —

OPPOSITE AND ABOVE RIGHT: The chestnut wood flooring defines the circulation path between the different areas while different flooring types, such as the tile in the dining area, help to create a unique zone. The stainless steel chairs, long narrow tables, and clean lines of the dining zone also differentiate it from the rest of the space. TOP: The central room is bounded on its long axis by a wood and stone paneled feature wall, patterned to resemble shingles or brickwork and express Boston's architectural vernacular. ABOVE LEFT: The traveler enters into the white reception area, where the walnut stained chestnut floor leads into the central room of the lounge.

Dining, Lounge, Business Center and Library. The space itself made fulfilling this requirement a challenge; it was small, long and narrow with no exterior light and surrounded by a public corridor. Adding further complications, explains Muhlfelder, *"there was an existing, functioning, airline lounge in the space at the start of the project, which prevented any research into existing conditions prior to design. Strict airport security posed its own unique challenges as site access was restricted."*

To differentiate the distinct areas within the Clubhouse and give each its own identity, the team varied the furniture, flooring, lighting and wall treatments and used chestnut wood flooring to define the circulation path between the areas. Strategic placement of LED lights throughout the space compensates for the total lack of natural light and creates a warm and inviting atmosphere.

Custom-made millwork casework actually forms the wall of the adjacent space, saving excess materials and money. Sustainable elements include the efficient lighting design which minimizes the overall number of lighting fixtures needed and the repurposed chestnut wood flooring. Efficient mechanical systems are designed with all of the supply placed at the center of the space and the return on the two ends.

Muhlfelder concludes, *"Bergmeyer worked closely with the lighting consultant, kitchen consultant, and the entire team to bring to life a space that responded to the client's needs and fulfilled the demands of air travelers."*

DESIGN: **Bergmeyer Associates, Inc.,** Boston, MA
LIGHTING: **Collaborative Lighting**
PHOTOGRAPHER: **Bruce T. Martin**

The neutral background palette is accented with bold red color and rich materials such as leather chairs and leather and mohair covered bench seating, expressing both the client's and Boston's culture while providing a warm, relaxing atmosphere.

super

markets

blt*supermarket

KKmall, Shenzhen, Guangdong Province, PR China

rkd retail/iQ

Bangkok/Shenzhen/Shanghai

ABOVE AND BELOW: Blt* supermarket's signature green color can't be missed from the aisle of the KKmall.

China Resources Vanguard (CRV) had the kind of problem all retailers should have — it's market-leading supermarket, Olé, was being courted by shopping center developers throughout China. The owners felt, however, that it was appropriate for Olé to be in only a limited number of shopping centers, yet many good spaces with significant potential were being offered and were of interest to CRV.

According to rkd retail/iQ, the firm responsible for the design of Olé, *"Rather than over extend and risk the Ole' brand, CRV agreed that it was time to develop a new format that could realize the broader opportunities and keep key new sites within the CRV family."* rkd retail/iQ were charged with designing the new brand, blt* supermarket, shown here.

rkd retail/iQ explains the name, *"blt*, an acronym for the China Resources service mark, "better life together" was created as a new-to-the-market format to be rolled out in Hong Kong and tier 1 and tier 2 cities in China. Although blt* will be brand consistent*

ABOVE AND BELOW: Dramatic, fresh architecture was developed around a store plan that emphasizes ease of shopping. Unique and attention-getting light fixtures are placed above key merchandise displays.

ABOVE AND LEFT: A large variety of merchandise is easily accessible in the wide aisles.

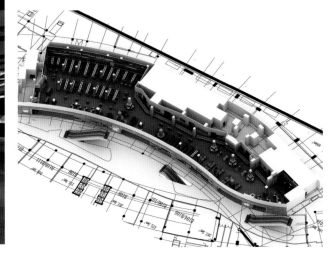

across both markets, the new segmented format will play different roles in each market. In Hong Kong, blt* will assume a CRC shop (+) position in terms of price and promotion within the consistent environmental design while in China, blt* will follow an Ole' (-) positioning. Both positioned formats will share a core range of merchandise and services that will be better than the competition with a clear price message." The blt* supermarket shown here is located in KKmall in Shenzhen and is 3,234 m2 (34,810 sq. ft.).

Dramatic architecture and the bright, green signature color beckon mall customers into the space.

Once inside, the store plan is designed to present merchandise categories in a way that allows for a variety of shopping patterns — from the quick stop to pick up a few items, to circulation throughout the store for the weekly shopping. Every shopper had to be able to easily meet his or her own needs.

rkd retail/iQ was responsible for the name generation, brand and environmental graphics, store planning and design and construction documents and the firm is currently rolling out blt* supermarkets across multiple locations in Hong Kong and China.

ABOVE AND BELOW: Categories such as deli and meats are clearly labeled including counters catering to quick stops to pick up lunch.

DESIGN: **rkd retail/iQ,** Bangkok, Shenzhen, Shanghai

CLIENT TEAM
DEPUTY CHAIRMAN AND CEO: **Long Chen**

CHIEF OPERATING OFFICER: **Hong Jie**

VICE PRESIDENT: **Qin Dong Sheng**

VICE PRESIDENT: **Kevin Chen**

GENERAL MANAGER: **Dai Hong**

DIRECTOR: **Ou Xueqing**

PHOTOGRAPHY: **Pruk Dejkamhang**

STORE SIZE: **3,234 m2** (34,810 sq. ft)

The interior of the new Blue Goose Market in St. Charles recalls the city's historic district in its boom years of the 1920s and '30s. Included are historic photographs and art deco touches that are consistent with the style of the city's revitalized waterfront.

For the interior, the designers specified vintage tin ceilings and a dyed concrete floor. The design of the store is in keeping with Blue Goose's reputation for old fashioned service and high-quality products.

DESIGN: **Store Design Services,** Minneapolis, MN

CREATIVE DIRECTOR: **Harry Steen**

SR. INTERIOR DESIGNER: **Molly Cade**

LEAD ARCHITECT: **Mike Klein**

PROJECT SUPERVISOR: **Shawn Rasmusen**

LIGHTING DESIGNER: **Terry Bright**

PROJECT MANAGER: **Mike Clayton**

PHOTOGRAPHY: **Martin Konopaki,** Chicago, IL

Bravo Supermercado

Santo Domingo, Dominican Republic

GHA design studios

GHA design studios was charged by Bravo Supermercado with designing not just a new, freestanding store, but a new supermarket experience — including a new company logo, packaging, labels and graphics — for the Santo Domingo market.

Debbie Kalisky, Director of Retail Development, explains, *"The goal was to try to differentiate Bravo from the local supermarket market. Before Bravo was built, the overwhelming majority of supermarkets in the Dominican Republic were overcrowded and poorly merchandised spaces. We wanted to introduce the local population to a European hypermarket concept of clean, cool lines while maintaining a Latin American cultural appeal through colors and graphics and remaining respectful of the value-consciousness of the local shopper. It was important to emphasize the Latin American aspect aesthetically."*

The resulting 25,000 sq. ft., multi-level space includes an underground parking area, a main selling floor and a mezzanine overlooking the checkout area. Exterior glazing the height of the building creates an open, inviting space, and allows clear views of the bold, red graphics, the escalator, and the lower-level parking area.

Inside, wide, uncluttered aisles permit stress-free cart mobility, while the clean lines of the fixtures — in white and black metal with little or no detailing — focus attention onto the merchandise. The produce area gets special attention thanks to a metal structure suspended from the ceiling with oversized circular cut-outs and cylindrical light fixtures.

Stylized graphics replace conventional signage and identify the different departments with pleasing colors and pictorial imagery. The greens and red-oranges of the graphics also appear as solid colors on select accent walls. Both the graphics and colors reappear at the checkout area where shoppers are able to get a peek at the pet shop on the mezzanine.

TOP: Strong branding and clean architectural volumes are introduced at the entrance. ABOVE: The escalator allows views of the underground parking level.

DESIGN: **GHA design studios**

ARCHITECT: **ARQ. R. Martinez & S. Hernandez; MyH Arquitectos,** Santo Domingo, R.D.

LIGHTING: **Amerlux,** Canton, OH

TILES: **Marazzi,** Sunnyvale, TX
Crossville, Virginia Tile Co, Livonia, MI

CUSTOM PANELS: **3Form,** Salt Lake City, UT

PHOTOGRAPHER: **Carlos Read**

TOP: On one wall, white, rigid board with circular cut-outs is offset in front of the background graphics, creating a peek-through effect.
ABOVE LEFT: Structured and systematic presentation ensures that products remain the focal point. **ABOVE RIGHT:** The orderly and clutter-free check out area.

Chedraui-Tepic

Tepic, Mexico

PDT International

Fort Lauderdale, Florida

Chedraui Supermarkets, one of Mexico's leading supermarket and hypermarket retailers, recently embarked on a campaign to revamp its store designs in an effort to reinforce its brand and expand its market share in the supermarket sector. It enlisted the help of PDT International to redesign its supermarket and hypermarket interiors and facades to provide a more shopper-friendly atmosphere, while at the same time reinforcing Chedraui's image as the place to shop for low-cost, high-quality groceries and assorted hard goods and merchandise.

Although the retailer's slogan, which can be found on the company logo, is *cuesta menos* — Spanish for "costs less" — part of the purpose behind the design initiative was to elevate the store's

ABOVE LEFT: Wide aisles throughout the store make for a more pleasant shopping experience. **ABOVE RIGHT:** The pet department is located in the center of the store and a high feature-wall with back-lit graphics draws the customer from any point within the store.

Circular discs suspended from the ceiling identify the deli meats department from afar and create an interesting visual and spatial relationship with the surrounding circular layout of the service areas.

Track lighting and custom fixtures showcase the international mix of wines and liquors in the wine shop, one of the main highlights of the store.

image to emphasize the high quality aspect of its message without in any way negating the brand's reputation as a low cost provider.

PDT International explains, *"The principal design goal was to create a more simplified layout and design for the typical Chedraui Supermarket that would create interesting and eye-catching instances that would provide for a more pleasurable shopping experience. One of the challenges was to do this without breaking the bank with expensive construction and finishes. Also, the store could not create the impression of an ostentatious, unnecessarily expensive store, offering goods beyond the target demographics budget range.*

"The design solution was ingenuously simple," continues someone, *"we reduced, and sometimes eliminated, the clutter of the traditional signage and frenzied goods displayed throughout the store. Departments are designed with clearly identifiable features that can be spotted from the moment the customer enters the store — from attention-grabbing graphics to encompassing floor finishes. Depart-*

ments were located strategically to attract shoppers to remote areas of the store, thereby increasing the chances of the impulse buy. The layout is fluid and concise, with ample aisles and low fixtures for a more open and inviting experience. All this was done while minimizing unnecessary construction, and employing attractive, affordable finishes to maintain the store brand's image of providing the lowest cost goods to a discerning customer."

The hypermarket in Tepic, shown here, is one of the first examples of the new store design and, since its opening, has enjoyed a huge success and marked increase in sales over similar stores. It's the prototype for all future Chedraui stores in similar markets.

The produce section includes large colorful graphics and strategically placed track lighting to highlight the fresh produce. The "dropped ceiling" of oversized leaves creates an intimate space-within-a-space, giving customers the feeling of shopping at a traditional farmers' market.

DESIGN: **PDT International,** Fort Lauderdale, FL

FIXTURES: **Ietsa**

LIGHTING: **PDT International**

STORE SIZE: **6,800 m2** (73,195 sq. ft.)

PHOTOGRAPHER: **Gabriel Raphael Franco**

Dave's Fresh Marketplace

Smithfield, Rhode Island

CIP Retail

Fairfield, Ohio

LEFT: The fresh fish counter is decorated with a mural depicting fishing boats.
OPPOSITE: The Apple Valley Food Barn recalls Smithfield's past as a major producer of apples.

Dave's Fresh Marketplace is the largest independent grocery chain in Rhode Island with nine stores throughout the state and a reputation for fresh, quality products and superior customer service. The chain evolved from a small roadside fruit and vegetable stand — Dave's Fruitland — opened by Dave Cesario in 1969.

In addition to its quality products and customer service, the market prides itself on its long-standing commitment to the communities it serves and strives to differentiate itself from the competition by incorporating elements into its stores that celebrate local history and architectural styles.

For instance, a Dave's Fresh Marketplace in Quonset, Rhode Island (designed by CIP Retail), is located near the ferry dock to Martha's Vineyard and has an interior design that emulates the architecture and store signage of the famous island.

For the recently-remodeled market shown here in Smithfield, the client asked CIP Retail to create a store with a rural feel that would capture the spirit and charm of Smithfield —a small New England town famous for its history of apple production and known locally as Apple Valley.

Within the store customers are met with references to the local character and architecture at

OPPOSITE: Various aspects of apple growing and production are featured in murals that surround the produce department. ABOVE: The aisle in front of The Cheese Lodge and The Delicatessen feel more like a small town street than a grocery store.

every turn. The shopping experience is more like walking from shop to shop in a small town than from department to department in a large grocery store.

The store's focal point is Apple Valley Food Barn, a faux barn the designers created to house the carving station, sushi bar, burrito and pasta stations and a brick pizza oven. The structure, which looks like someone built a small barn right in the store, stands, of course, near the apples, and comes complete with a typical New England roof line, aged-looking red boards and even a hay loft.

The Apple Valley Food Barn is not, however, the only structure within the store that resembles a building. The row of cash registers is sheltered under a "roadside stand" with weather-worn planking and a "tin roof" overhang and, nearby, the customer service counter is housed in a quaint, cottage-like structure. The Cheese Lodge and The Delicatessen sit next to each other and boast overhead facades that resemble small town storefronts.

In keeping with the market's dedication to fresh

food and its beginnings as a roadside stand, the produce department received special attention. Around the bulkhead and between sturdy-looking barn "beams" and "rafters" are murals depicting Smithfield's historic orchards and apple production. The fixtures and flooring in the department continue the rough-hewn look. Other murals around the store include a fishing boat scene in the seafood department and cooking utensils above the prepared foods counter.

CIP Retail was responsible for all facets of the store's 35,000 square-foot interior, including flooring, lighting, interior construction, branding, wayfinding and installation — and, adding to the challenge, they completed the project in just four months.

Everywhere one looks in Dave's Fresh Marketplace structures and imagery, both large and small, pay homage to the town of Smithfield.

Customer's check out under the protective awning of a "roadside stand" — a nod to the retailer's origins as a roadside fruit and vegetable stand.

DESIGN: **CIP Retail,** Fairfield, OH

STORE SIZE: **3,252 m2** (35,000 sq. ft.)

PHOTOGRAPHER: **Nick Graham Photography**

Landmark Supermarket

Landmark Department Store, Manila, Philippines

Hugh Boyd Architects
Montclair, New Jersey

OPPOSITE: The seating areas of the supermarket's food court are separated from the main circular aisles by a railing construction of one-inch thick acrylic with oval decorations.

The Landmark Department store in Manila is a famous name and this new store — the first in 30 years — is located at the terminus of Manila's main rapid transit line in the area known as Trinoma. The supermarket is situated in the building's basement and consists of 94,000 square feet of supermarket space with 68 checkouts, and an additional 35,000 square feet of warehouse space. There's a food court that features 34 food vendors and can seat 1,400 patrons.

According to Hugh Boyd, the architect/designer of the space, *"Early in the construction of the store, a series of structural columns had to be reinforced with large, low hanging armatures. A major decorative effect was created by wrapping these columns in bowl-shaped fabrications, upon which images of local fruits and flowers were abstracted and painted."*

A series of curved pathways, along with two vendor kiosks, break up the seating area in the food court into smaller, more intimate groupings. The seating areas are separated from the main circular aisles by a railing construction of one-inch thick solid acrylic with oval decorations. The designs were routed in the field.

Interest at the ceiling, and a sense of spaciousness, is created with a series of light-colored, loating planes suspended from the exposed ceiling structure, which was painted a dark color to add depth.

Since electricity is very expensive in the Philippines, stores are usually illuminated at much lower levels. Further adding to the lighting challenge is a complete lack of natural light. According to the designers, *"The design strategy was to brightly light vertical surfaces and critical displays using energy efficient metal halide and fluorescent light fixtures, while keeping the overall general lighting levels low. This approach led the specialty departments in the supermarket and the vendor spaces in the food court to become the theatrical focus of both spaces."*

The scarcity of wood in the Philippines means that the use of wood is both restricted and expensive. *"Our response to this challenge was to base the majority of the design upon inexpensive painted gypsum board, fiberglass reinforced gypsum shapes and a locally produced solid surface acrylic material similar to Corian."*

The results are sleek and contemporary.

A ceiling structure of suspended planes in various shapes adds interest throughout the store. The overall lighting level is low with dramatic highlights on the critical displays.

DESIGN: **Hugh Boyd Architects,** Montclair, NJ
Hugh Boyd FAIA, A. Henderson Boyd, Jo Ann Montero

LANDMARK CONSTRUCTION TEAM
HEAD OF CONSTRUCTION: **David Go**

SENIOR PROJECT MANAGER: **Arlene Encinas**

HEAD OF ENGINEERING: **Noel Tolin**

HEAD OF STORE PLANNING: **Norman Manalo**

TEAM: **Nolan Llanora, Reymand Javier, Ronalyn Pitogo**

PHOTOGRAPHY: **Toto Labrador,** Quezon City, Philippines

Longo's
Maple Leaf Square, Toronto

Watt International, Inc.
Toronto

Watt International was recently tasked with the design of the new Longo's supermarket, located on the lower level of Toronto's Maple Leaf Square. The client wanted to take advantage of the high visibility of the downtown location to achieve strong sells, develop customer loyalty and position themselves effectively against key competitors. Longo's passion for fresh food had to be communicated through the design, as did its long and respected heritage in the Toronto community.

The first challenge the designers had to overcome was simply to get customers down to the lower level and into the store itself. To do this, they utilized the attention-getting wonders of technology and surrounded the store's main entryway, a set of escalators, with animation depicting the store's many fresh offerings and food preparation. In addition, an electronic billboard, easily read by anyone descending the escalators, advertises in-store specials, promotions and events. And finally, suspended from the ceiling, is a "bushel basket" reminding customers of Longo's long-standing dedication to fresh-from-the-

OPPOSITE: Customers are enticed down the escalators with animation, an electronic billboard and an overhead "bushel basket" with the Longo's logo. ABOVE: The produce department features, in addition to the vibrancy of the fruit and vegetables themselves, bulkhead shadow-boxes with a "fresh-from-the-field" message in the form of wheat in sculptural relief. Both bushel basket and wheat fields remind consumers of Longo's dedication to fresh food.

OPPOSITE AND BELOW: The perishable products on display in the salad bar and prepared food areas are made more appetizing and given heighten appeal by the gleaming stainless steel fixtures. Overhead labels, with clear typography, allow the fixtures to be identified from a distance.

field — or from-the-orchard — produce. LED lights within the basket change color to emulate what's in season, for instance red during apple season.

The irregular footprint of the store and the space's many columns posed another challenge — this one met with careful store planning. Strategic "destinations" were created throughout the space to let customers move logically from one area to the next, allowing for intuitive shopping patterns. The columns were wrapped in graphics, turning them from hindrances into valuable communication points.

Yet, another challenge was the multiple entry points from Maple Leaf Square. In addition to the main escalators, elevators and stairs from parking garages and secondary entrances lead to the lower level, and made clearly defining the store's control points and circulation patterns difficult. To avoid building walls the designers utilized way-finding signs, custom merchandising fixtures and strategic placement of the checkout counters to guide customers through the space.

The completed store possesses a level of sophistication more common to a high-end supermarket than in a competitively-priced market such as Longo's. Contributing to this polished character, in addition to the intelligent store layout and elegant custom-designed fixtures, are Longo's many unique features. A green, "living" wall of plants strengthens the retailers "fresh" and "green" messages while acting as a natural indoor air filter system. Sending a slightly different message, but equally unique, is a faux chocolate column that looks like a huge floor-to-ceiling chocolate bar and reminds any passing chocolaholic that the object of his or her addiction is available close by.

High on the walls in the produce department shadow boxes with "wheat field" displays remind consumers that food isn't manufactured in grocery stores, while graphics throughout the space complement the architecture and reinforce brand's messages.

ABOVE: A "chocolate" column, complete with audio/visual inserts, ensures the chocolatier won't be missed. **OPPOSITE:** Custom fixtures in the cheese and deli department and the meat and seafood counter guide customers and display fresh food to its best advantage. A black board behind the meat counter illustrates various cuts of meat.

A "living wall" not only brands Longo's "fresh" message, it also acts as a natural air filtration system.

DESIGN: **Watt International, Inc.,** Toronto, ON, Canada

Watt International Design Team

TEAM LEAD, INTERIOR DESIGN: **Glen Kerr**

INTERIOR DESIGN: **Paulis Ciskevicius, Sam Chan**

ILLUSTRATION: **Matt DeAbreu**

GRAPHICS: **Bryan Morris, Ash Pabani, Eliza Tang**

PROJECT MANAGEMENT: **Shahla Mulji,** Account Manager

Other Resources

ARCHITECT: **Stephen Pile Architect Inc.,** Toronto, ON

GENERAL CONTRACTOR: **RFB Construction,** Burlington, ON

LIGHTING: **Jordan Architectural Group Ltd.,** Toronto, ON

SIGNAGE: **Canadian Sign Systems,** Port Perry, ON

PLANT WALL: **Nedlaw Living Walls,** Breslau, ON

PHOTOGRAPHY: **Si Hoang,** Toronto, ON

ABOVE: Leaving no opportunity to send the Longo's two most important messages go by, the designers covered the parking garage elevator doors with images of fresh fields and brand heritage. BELOW: Corks, a local beer and wine bar located within the store, gives customers a convenient and comfortable place to relax.

Pusateri's

Bayview Village, Toronto

GHA design studios

The store has three entrances, two from the mall and one exterior. One of the mall entrances serves as a sort of "concierge" desk.

With this new space, Pusateri's — a well-loved food emporium of fine imported Italian and prepared foods — takes its first foray into a mall location after two previous store openings.

As envisioned by the design team of GHA design studios, a contemporary approach was taken for the gourmet food shop and, according to the designers, an environment was created of *"clean architectural lines and materials — treated monolithically."* Food as Fashion was the guiding principle in the design approach. Carrera marble, limestone and dark stained wood serve as *"a luxurious background for the artfully arranged merchandise to be presented."*

Pusateri's has two entrances from the mall and one from the exterior. One of the mall entrances is treated as a sort of hotel registration or concierge desk, with the Carrera marble slabs contrasting

with the dramatic, dark wood. The other mall entrance leads directly into the produce section. This area is highlighted with a woven textured ceiling and architectural lighting set within wooden troughs. This is a self-contained section of the store and the ceiling treatment helps to distinguish it.

Throughout the space there are highlighted areas. Fine olives and oils, and their accompanying lines, are arranged within dark wood and stainless steel fixtures. Polished, circular decorative chrome light fixtures inject a fashion vibe into the environment. Also adding to the upscale look of Pusateri's are the reflective glass and stone surfaces, an aesthetic often found in high end fashion department stores.

Shopping Pusateri's is like wandering through

an up-scale European department store food hall. It's elegant, smart and sophisticated. The product display is top-of-the-line to complement the top grade of the products.

The overall lighting scheme flatters both the merchandise and the shoppers and gives the space a pleasant ambience. White walls and dark wood and stainless steel accents, complete the picture of a modern food shop.

Food is Fashion was the guiding principle of the design — Carrera marble, limestone and dark stained wood serve as luxurious backdrops for the artfully arranged merchandise.

DESIGN: **GHA Studio**

PARTNER: **Frank Di Niro**

PROJECT DIRECTOR: **James Lee**

SENIOR DESIGNER: **Lily Yuan**

STORE SIZE: **929 m2 (**10,000 sq. ft.)

PHOTOGRAPHY: **Philip Castleton,** Toronto, ON, Canada

Ole'

Holiday Plaza Shopping Center, Shenzhen, Guangdong Province, PR China

rkd retail/iQ

Bangkok, Shenzhen, Shanghai

Ole' generation two, shown here, is a unifying and momentum-building brand evolution of what was the single most important lifestyle supermarket brand in China, Ole'. The original Ole' brand proved that the concept of an upscale supermarket in China was a viable idea, as traffic and sales performance exceeded all expectations.

The goal of rkd retail/iQ, when concepting Ole' generation two, was to create a merchandise- and customer service driven–experience, with the designed environment assuming a secondary role. The entire Ole' concept was reevaluated from the merchandise level out. Categories were combined and the logo refined to enhance the lifestyle and up-market positioning of the brand and to differentiate Ole' generation two from the competition, including the original Ole markets.

That competition was threatening to confuse the Ole' image as other supermarkets opened, and Ole' generation one supermarkets were being implemented by other regional divisions of the parent company, China Resources Vanguard, without the same level of discipline and refinement that existed in the original Ole' flagship location.

With the creation of this Ole' in the Holiday Plaza Shopping Center the momentum of the original store was regained and the brand objectives realigned.

TOP: Ole' as seen from the Holiday Plaza Shopping Center. ABOVE: The lighting scheme incorporates a variety of indirect, internally illuminated and general illumination to create dramatic lighting effects that add interest and highlights.

The high quality of the fresh fruits and vegetables on offer is literally reflected in overhead architectural elements and figuratively reflected in the larger-than-life branding imagery.

DESIGN: **rkd retail/iQ,** Bangkok, Shenzhen, Shanghai

STORE SIZE: **5,240m2** (56,400 sq. ft.)

CLIENT TEAM
DEPUTY CHAIRMAN AND CEO: **Long Chen**

CHIEF OPERATING OFFICER: **Hong Jie**

VICE PRESIDENT: **Qin Dong Sheng**

VICE PRESIDENT: **Kevin Chen**

GENERAL MANAGER: **Dai Hong**

DIRECTOR: **Ou Xueqing**

GENERAL MANAGER: **Dai Hong**

PHOTOGRAPHY: **Pruk Dejkamhang**

ABOVE AND BELOW: Clear merchandising with a focus on the depth and variety of products is the simple philosophy of Ole'. As most of the imported products are new to the Chinese consumer, clarity of display is key to self-education and selection. Brand, category, product benefits, price and promotion graphics were all developed to support the upscale and lifestyle positioning of Ole'.

Located in the central hub of the new plan are fresh food categories of Asian and Western delis, meat, fish/seafood, diary and fruit/vegetable, while key positioning categories such as wine/tobacco, trend/gift and café/bakery are near the main entrance. The overall customer flow offers multiple circulation patterns and touch points to encourage shoppers to take their time with the many offerings.

The materials and color palettes change according to the merchandise category. Warmer materials such as wood are utilized for coffee/café, bakery, and Western and Asian deli, while more dramatic materials such as brushed copper and aluminum ceiling tiles can be found in the meat, fish, dairy and frozen food categories. Throughout the store full-color lifestyle photography was chosen to enhance the architecture.

rkd retail/iQ was responsible for the strategic brief, all creative expressions, name generation, brand and environmental graphic programs and retail planning plus design and construction documentation. Ole' is currently being implemented into upscale locations throughout China.

ABOVE: Health, beauty and cosmetics, complete with overhead graphics, is located near a secondary mall entrance. **BELOW:** At the check out counters all elements are geared for branding, customer service and convenience.

Ralph's Food Warehouse

Rio Grande, Puerto Rico

CIP Retail

Fairfield, Ohio

Ralph's Food Warehouse, one of the most progressive and well-known grocery operators in Puerto Rico, recently put its best foot forward with a new, 52,000 square-foot store in Rio Grande. The company operates eight Ralph's stores and two Supermercados Del Este grocery stores on the island.

The sleek new design concept for Rio Grande — developed by CIP Retail of Fairfield, Ohio — includes state-of-the-art equipment, the latest lighting technology and abundant skylights. The resulting environment caters to a large volume of customers with ease, while focusing everyone's attention onto the food.

The feeling of the space is one of openness and light. The high ceiling and its visible structure are painted white and interspersed with skylights that allow natural light to flood the space. Further brightening the interior is the light, natural and not, that bounces off the white floors.

The color palette is a sophisticated mix of white and various shades of yellow and orange with accent points of warm, dark red and subtle gray/greens.

Large, close-up photographs of the tasty offerings are placed in the appropriate departments, both directly above product displays and on the walls. Additional graphics in stylized food patterns can be found on vertical wayfinding signs and accent panels in the large eat-in cafeteria. In addition, departments are clearly labeled with dimensional typography that curves from the bulkheads.

One of the predominant elements of the design can be found at the checkout area. Suspended above the registers are custom-designed accent panels that form a canopy overhead — creating an interesting perspective and reducing the scale of the space as customers check out. Although the panels have a very dimensional, even heavy, appearance, they are actually lightweight foam core panels laminated with printed Sintra sheets, each weighing only about 35 pounds.

The finished store is clean and vibrant — an enjoyable environment for Ralph's loyal clientele and new customers alike.

OPPOSITE: The yellow and orange color scheme complements the colorful products in the produce department, while large photos of the tasty offerings draw in customers. ABOVE: The frozen foods aisle glistens as light streams in from skylights and reflects off the display cases and the floor.

ABOVE: Curved typography can be found throughout the store. In some departments the bulkhead walls curve, while elsewhere it's the type itself that extends from its base. **OPPOSITE TOP:** The panels above the check out counters, although substantial in appearance, only weigh about 35 pounds each. **OPPOSITE BOTTOM:** A large eat-in cafeteria continues the sophisticated design of the store.

DESIGN: **CIP Retail,** Fairfield, OH
STORE SIZE: **4,831 m2** (52,000 sq. ft.)
PHOTOGRAPHER: **Alise O'Brien Photography**

Roche Bros.

West Borough, Massachuetts

FRCH Design Worldwide
Cincinnati, Ohio

The Boston supermarket chain Roche Bros. invited FRCH Worldwide Design to *"develop a fresh outlook" for their stores while "retaining the essence of their proud heritage"* in the increasingly competitive grocery market. The result is shown here in the store built in West Borough. The design concept story, as imagined by the designers at FRCH, was that Roche Bros. had taken over an historic mill building and that core offerings were being presented as if by vendors in an indoor market.

The new design, according to the designers, *celebrates fresh appeal reminiscent of Boston marketplaces and leverages the Roche Bros. history through the messaging and imagery that reinforce the brand promise."* The designers worked with the Roche Bros. team *"to take a pictorial, organic position in botanicals within their storewide graphic system, starting with in-house employees' illustrations that were used as the bases to create the final artwork and environmental graphic designs."* The botanical

drawings — in black and white line drawings — appear on fascias and soffits around the specialty shops as well as on the kiosks and food stands out on the floor.

The material palette throughout the store also remained true and consistent with the "old mill" concept. There are wood planked floors, areas of walls sheathed in wood, brick or stone, and brick and stone work used in other areas to continue the natural, earthy look. In the all-important produce zone, natural light was utilized *"to create hero fixtures reminiscent of a market square."*

While developing a fresh perspective for their client, the designers — with this new/old concept — retained and enhanced Roche Bros. essence and their proud heritage. The increase in sales in some key service offerings proves that the public has more than accepted this new/old look.

ABOVE AND BELOW: Rough stone is used to create a major design element in the salad bar area and several of the island food stands rest on pedestals of layered brick. Featured throughout the store are graphics based on drawings by store employees.

In the frozen foods aisle, the cases in the center were lowered and clerestory lighting was used to turn the dark, gray tunnel of refrigerated cases into a welcoming, open vista.

DESIGN: **FRCH Design Worldwide,** Cincinnati, OH

VP, MANAGING CREATIVE DIRECTOR: **Andrew McQuilkin**

DESIGN DIRECTOR: **Young Rok Park**

SENIOR INTERIOR DESIGNER: **Lis Diaz, LEED AP**

SENIOR GRAPHIC DESIGNER: **Mike Juras**

SENIOR RESOURCE DESIGNER: **Carol Osterbrock, LEED AP**

SENIOR DESIGNER: **Hee Sun Kim**

INTERIOR DESIGNERS: **Nicki Dubois, Heather Storer, Holly Trucco**

STORE SIZE: **4,459 m2** (48,000 sq. ft.)

Whole Foods Market

Venice, California

Studio One Eleven

Long Beach, California

The Lincoln & Rose shopping center in Venice, California was badly in need of renovation. Originally built in the 1960s, the nondescript shopping center was plagued with awkward additions, an influx of low-rent tenants, crime and general disrepair.

Combined Properties, Inc. (CPI), the owner and developer of the site, entered into an agreement with Whole Foods Market to lease a majority of the property and, in conjunction with the market, the development team took a "master planning" approach to the redevelopment of the site. Studio One Eleven was brought onboard with the goal of creating a design-intense project which would generate a "sense of place" within the underserved community. The goal was to transform the center into a community gathering place.

Although interior spaces were modified to accommodate the large-scale supermarket anchor, demolition was minimized. The original canopy of the building was removed and many of the building materials

Close attention was paid to the details to add a layer of complexity, giving the building a strong presence from the street.

LEFT: Expanded sidewalks allow for the garden center and outdoor patio to serve as gathering places for the community. RIGHT: Exterior lighting is used to encourage evening activity.

were installed directly over the existing façade. The new, distinctive building exterior established an inviting atmosphere, while reflecting the unique character of Venice Beach.

The materials palette included stucco, steel, metal panels and wood siding. As Alan Pullman, AIA, Senior Principal of Studio One Eleven, explains, *"The exterior aesthetic is contemporary, yet appropriate for the context of a beach community. Close attention was paid to the details to add a layer of complexity, giving the building a strong presence from the street and an up-close tactile feel. The sidewalk design was inspired by the beach, including decorative concrete with shell and pebble aggregate."*

The sidewalks were expanded by approximately 10 feet to accommodate pedestrian traffic and the various outdoor uses such as Whole Foods Market's garden center and outdoor dining patio. Exterior lighting emphasizes the architectural features, accents plants, and encourages evening activity. After closing, the exterior

sales area is secured by lowering the façade's innovative mechanized metal and wood gate. When lowered, it exposes a series of green and blue glass panels.

The project incorporated many sustainable initiatives. In addition to using products containing recycled content wherever possible, sustainable components of the overall site included a bio-swale/filtration system to treat storm water run-off, reduced site lighting and LEED® TI certification for the Whole Foods Market interior. Landscaping included drought tolerant and native plants and 60 new trees in the parking area to shade cars and reduce the heat-island effect of asphalt paving.

"Since opening," states Pullman, *"Whole Foods has performed beyond expectations and is the leading store in the chain's Western Region. The store and development has been utilized by Whole Foods as a case study for future development by the company and has been meticulously reviewed to determine how to replicate its success."*

RIGHT: The distinct and innovative mechanized metal and wood gate secures the exterior sales area after closing.
BELOW: Ample outdoor space allows the display of fresh fruits and vegtables.

DESIGN: **Studio One Eleven,** Long Beach, CA

DEVELOPER: **Combined Properties, Inc.**

FIXTURES

   IPE WOOD, CEDAR, BAMBOO PLYWOOD: **Royal Plywood**

   GALVANIZED WEATHERING STEEL, SHEET METAL: **Bischoff Sheet Metal**

   GLASS: **Oldcastle Glass**

   STOREFRONT - ARCADIA: **Breezeway Thrifty Glass**

   STUCCO - OMEGA COLORTEK: **Richmond Plastering**

   STEEL: **Access Steel Fabricators**

   PAINTING: **Rossi Painting**

   CONCRETE FLATWORK: **Pave West**

   MASONRY - ORCO BLOCK: **Juarez Masonry & Concrete**

   ROOFING - GAF 4-PLY BUR: **Alliance Roofing Company**

   WATERPROOFING - TREMCO TREMPROOF 201 & 250: **Mark Beamish Waterproofing**

   VERTICAL LIFT GATES: **California Automatic Gate and Door Enterprise**

LIGHTING: **USA Architectural Lighting**

LANDSCAPING: **Silver Oaks Landscaping**

GENERAL CONTRACTOR: **AJ Padelford**

STRUCTURAL: **VLG Engineering**

CIVIL: **Hall & Foreman**

LANDSCAPE ARCHITECT: **EPT Design**

ELECTRICAL: **Nikolakopulos & Associates**

SIGNAGE DESIGNER: **Newsom Design**

LAND USE CONSULTANT: **Craig Lawson & Co., LLC**

INTERIORS: **DL English Design Studio**

PHOTOGRAPHY: **Tom Bonner Photography**

food
retailers

& markets

Arabesq

Dubai Mall, UAE

Part of ABU ISSA HOLDING
Doha-Qater

Arabesq, a confectionery in Dubai Mall, offers a diverse range of high-end oriental sweets from major locations within the Arabic world, such as Lebanon, Syria, Jordan, Morocco, Tunis, Oman, Qatar and UAE. Available for the first time outside Syria is Bekdash, one of the finest handmade ice creams in the Middle East. At Arabesq customers can enjoy the traditional ice cream and taste the finest ice cream flavors of the region. The shop will also fulfill special orders and deliver anywhere in the UAE.

Upon entering the shop customers are met with a mid-floor display comprised of a grouping of display units arranged to resemble a dining table — recalling to mind the gracious hospitality for which the Middle East is famous. Painted a glossy white the units have copper and aluminum inlays and several also feature white marble. Overhead a large, golden chandelier is suspended from a soffit with a central reflective area that adds sparkle to the displays.

Wall display units along the sides and back of the store are also painted a glossy white and the products they showcase are illuminated with backlighting and mirrors placed inside the shelves. Underfoot, mosaic tiles in a brass-like color cover the front of the store while epoxy resin in rich chocolate brown adds depth and an alluring sheen to the sales area in back.

Highlighting the products and reflecting off the high-gloss surfaces is light from track lights, medium and wide beam down lights, cove lighting and custom-designed pendant lights made from copper-platted aluminum.

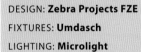

DESIGN: **Zebra Projects FZE**
FIXTURES: **Umdasch**
LIGHTING: **Microlight**
STORE SIZE: **132 m2** (1,421 sq. ft.)

The entire space and its tempting products sparkle and shine between the blacked-out ceiling and the rich depths of the epoxy floor. Highlights of bronze and copper abound.

Bob Evans Taste of the Farm

Westville, Ohio

Chute Gerdeman

Columbus, Ohio

Bob Evans family-friendly restaurants are noted for their wholesome foods. Elle Chute, Principal at Chute Gerdeman design firm explains, *"Bob Evans restaurants have a fierce brand loyalty among consumers. It was a natural evolution to expand the offer into a retail food environment, where carry-out customers can pick up menu favorites and meals for their whole families. By telling the retail story via seasonal, delicious flavors, the offer is constantly refreshed, and new avenues for product development can be explored."*

In keeping with the ever expanding trend towards carry-out meals, the Bob Evans group asked Chute Gerdeman to *"launch a retail and carry-out concept in line with existing restaurant settings providing convenient meal solutions for family as well as 'grab and go' options. Most importantly, keep Bob Evans' signature delicious seasonal flavors front and center."*

The new concept, Taste of the Farm, is a natural extension of the restaurant setting as the existing lobby and waiting room has been repurposed into

DESIGN:
Chute Gerdeman, Columbus, OH

CO-FOUNDER & CEO:
Dennis Gerdeman

CO-FOUNDER & PRINCIPAL:
Elle Chute

DIRECTOR, PROGRAM MANAGEMENT:
Cindy McCoy

DIRECTOR, BRAND STRATEGY:
Mindi Trank

DIRECTOR, BRAND COMMUNICATIONS:
Jay Highland

DESIGNER, BRAND COMMUNICATIONS:
Mary Lynn Penner

SR. DESIGNER, GRAPHIC IMPLEMENTATION:
Steve Johnson

DESIGNER, MATERIALS SPECIALIST:
Katie Clements

PHOTOGRAPHY: **Brandon L. Jones**
Columbus, OH
www.brandonljones.com

a retail experience. Key customer touch points have been created: a bakery offer, cold case "grab and go" items, family meals, self-service coffee, retail items and a catering service.

The Taste of the Farm carry-out shop also has a distinct and separate entry so that items can be picked up quickly and conveniently. On the wall behind the seating area, the Bob Evans brand story is illustrated. *"The Bob Evans farm background remains a constant while residential framed images change out on a seasonal basis reiterating the delicious flavors that come from 'down on the farm.'"*

On the left side of the space are the "grab and

go" case, coffee service and the pantry items, while a central core presentation is made for family meals and bakery selections. The off-white cabinetry and built-in refrigerated cases set against the soft, sunny yellow walls are all reminders of the brand's farm kitchen background. The warm and cozy ambiance is further reinforced by the wood floor laid in a chevron pattern.

This prototype is in a suburb of Columbus and has proven so successful that a rollout is in effect.

Canyon Market

Hyatt Regency Scottsdale Resort, Scottsdale, Arizona

Mars Solutions
Carlsbad, California

Hyatt Regency Scottsdale Resort and Spa, in Scottsdale, Arizona, was recently tasked with converting an old concierge office at the resort into Canyon Market, a 24-hour "grab and go" lifestyle store offering food, beverages and the gear necessary to enjoy Arizona's many outdoor activities. Of paramount importance to the client was sustainability — a concept practiced via many green initiatives at the resort.

The designers were directed to select recycled and sustainable products whenever possible in designing the space, and source products that would complement the resort's location, lifestyle and ideals.

Since the finished market is extremely small, only 83.6 m2, and sells a diverse range of products — pastries and hiking shorts; salads and shoulder bags; wine and bananas — the challenge was to create an integrated environment. The colors and theme of the design were enlisted to act as unifiers, allowing the disparate products to coexist without feeling forced or disjointed.

The rich, warm earth tones and interesting textures of the American Southwest can be found everywhere — in the color palette, graphics, materials and finishes.

What appears to be worn-looking wood on the floor is actually ceramic tiles, the walls are bamboo, and the countertop is recycled glass and stone. Adding interest to the ceiling is a suspended wood trellis custom designed for the project and inspired by the geometric designs of Frank Lloyd Wright. Hanging above the counter are lighting fixtures selected for their Southwestern aesthetic as well as the fact that they're made from recycled materials.

The resulting space is entirely consistent with the look and philosophy of the resort and the surrounding landscape, and truly reflects the motto found on the market's front sign: "Eat, Drink, Hike, Repeat."

DESIGN: **indidesign,** Los Angeles, CA
RETAIL CONSULTANT: **Mars Solutions,** Carlsbad, CA
SIZE: **83.5 m2** (900 sq. ft.)
FIXTURES: **Holiday Foliage,** San Diego, CA

While Canyon Market sells many eco-sensitive products, special emphasis is given to the reusable water bottles, part of the resort's "no plastic water bottle campaign" which offers guests who purchase reusable bottles unlimited free water refills. These bottles are front and center. Other eco-sensitive products include shoulder bags made from recycled magazines and burlap; notebooks made from paper and rice bags; and souvenir glass made from the resort's empty wine bottles.

Cioccolatitaliani

Milan

Costa Group
Riccò del Golfo, La Spezia, Italy

LEFT: The busy location is right down the street from the Milan Cathedral, attracting a booming take-out trade. **ABOVE:** Large windows bring the ambience of the street into the store and allow passersby a glimpse of the behind-the-counter action.

This, the second Cioccolatitaliani operation in Milan, recently opened on Via San Raffaele, one of the most desirable streets in the city, and just a few steps away from the Duomo Milano, or the Milan Cathedral and Square. Taking advantage of the high-traffic, high-visibility location, the store enjoys a robust take-out business and caters to both tourists and locals, selling a wide variety of chocolates, ice cream, pastries, coffee and sandwiches.

This location, like the other, was designed by Costa Group, an Italian firm with extensive

experience in the food retail sector. The format for Cioccolatitaliani's success is based its ability to delivery authenticity, originality and a genuine Italian product in an environment that allows the product to be the star. It's imperative to the retail that everything sold be consistently of the highest quality.

The focal point of the space is a long counter and all the enticing items it dispenses and displays, including its dipping wells for ice cream, coffee machine, chocolate fountain, and display cabinets

for pastries and sandwiches. The warm colors and materials used throughout the space — the wood of the floor, the stone covering the counter and the white pottery and kitchen tiles — all reflect the many shades of the varieties of chocolate that fill the store.

The retailer's motto, *noi lo facciamo davanti a tutti* — which loosely translates "we prepare your food in front of everyone" or perhaps even more loosely "we have nothing to hide" — is an indication of its dedication to transparency. Cioccolatitaliani ignores the tradition of keeping back-of-house activities hidden from public view and places all food preparation and manufacture within the sight of everyone in the store, as well as passersby on the street.

ABOVE: The main counter, and focal point of the shop, is made of rough stone and dramatically lit from the floor.
RIGHT: The concept of transparency is important at Cioccolatitaliani, all food preparation and manufacture is carried out in full view of the public. Their motto, *"noi lo facciamo davanti a tutti"* — which loosely translates "we prepare your food in front of everyone" is emblazed on a counter.

DESIGN: **Costa Group,**
Riccò del Golfo, La Spezia, Italy

PHOTOGRAPHY: ©**Costagroup.net**

Cowgirl Creamery Sidekick

The Ferry Building Marketplace, San Francisco

BALDAUF CATTON VON ECKARTSBERG Architects
San Francisco

The front display and service counter runs the full width of the long, narrow retail space. Cowgirl Creamery's artisan cheeses are front and center.

Cowgirl Creamery, an acclaimed maker of artisan cheeses with a retail operation in San Francisco's Ferry Building, was facing a growing demand for prepared cheese and dairy products. Taking advantage of a vacancy next door to their retail operation, the company tasked BALDAUF CATTON VON ECKARTSBERG Architects to design of Cowgirl Creamery Sidekick. The new "Sidekick" offers an array of dairy-based to-go goods, such as breakfast sandwiches, a fresh mozzarella bars, yogurt bowls, cottage cheese and hot and cold milk drinks.

The new jewel-box, 35 m2 space has the ability to merchandise and serve from both the front and the side of the high-traffic location in the central passage of the Ferry Building.

Across the front of the long, narrow shop, BCV created a full-width display case to maximize product display and serving efficiency. Reclaimed blue-gum eucalyptus vertical planks enclose the counter and highlight the entire space. Around the corner, a dramatically wood-framed side opening functions as a "Milk Bar" for quick pickup of hot and cold drinks for the rush of incoming morning ferry commuters.

Yellow is featured prominently, in tile work and on cabinets — here on the raclette station at the front counter.

The side opening enables Sidekick to cater, at lightning speed, to commuters rushing through the Ferry Building. The wood is reclaimed blue-gum eucalyptus and locally sourced.

Important to owner and client, Sue Conley, was the utilization of artisan craftspeople of Marin County, where her cheese-making business is based. Tiled walls are by Sausalito-based Heath Ceramics — a neighbor in the Ferry Building. The company provided the handmade cream and yellow tiles and unveiled their new Dwell Patterns half-hex tiles in a pattern created by BCV. In addition, wood-planked walls and elm slab countertops feature the work of West Marin sawyer Evan Shively, and are sourced from local urban forests.

The owner has also built community among her Ferry Building neighbors: Sidekick serves a San Francisco egg cream made with a special chocolate from Ferry Building tenant Michael Recchiuti of Recchiuti Confections.

Marin County-based Heath Ceramics provided the tiles, both the cheery yellow and cream tiles and the Dwell Patterns created by BCV in its first public use.

DESIGN: **BALDAUF CATTON VON ECKARTSBERG Architects,** San Francisco, CA

TILE: **Heath Ceramics,** Sausalito, CA

RECLAIMED WOOD: **Arborica,** Petaluma, CA, **Evan Shively**

PHOTOGRAPHER: **Mariko Reed**

Eataly

Genoa, Italy

Costa Group

Riccò del Golfo, La Spezia, Italy

ABOVE LEFT: The ice cream shop is near the entrance. **ABOVE RIGHT:** The fish area offers a sit-down meal or a fish to go.

Eataly is a concept developed by Oscar Farinetti to showcase the fine foods and wines for which Italy is famous. With locations in Turin, Tokyo, New York and Genoa, shown here, Farinetti's *"Temples to Made-in-Italy"* bring together, under one roof, stalls and shops offering a wide range of the finest Italian foods and wine, as well as multiple dining areas in which to enjoy a snack or meal — much like a traditional market, but with all of the conveniences of modern store and restaurant design.

Eataly Genoa is located between the historic Pirates' Galleon and the modern Aquarium in the picturesque Porto Antico (or Old Harbor), and has fast become a destination for tourists and locals alike. As in other Eataly locations, Italy's Costa Group was responsible for the design of the fixtures and furnishings, carefully designing each element to display the featured items in an appro-priate manner while maintaining an overall look consistent with the duel Italian traditions of great food and impeccable design sensibilities.

Eataly Genoa covers 1,600 m2 and includes meat, seafood and vegetable markets, restaurants, a cheese tasting area, a café and a chocolate shop. Consumers have the option of either carrying out the products to prepare a meal at home or consuming them in dining areas on the premises — a place for gourmands to enjoy each other's company and indulge their desire for fine food and wine.

Costa Group and Eataly plan on moving forward together with new locations.

DESIGN: **Costa Group,**
Riccò del Golfo, La Spezia, Italy
PHOTOGRAPHY: ©**Costagroup.net**

TOP LEFT: A magnificent harbor view is never far away. **ABOVE LEFT:** A traditional oven in the pizzeria. **ABOVE RIGHT:** That basic ingredient of Italian cooking, olive oil, is available in its own corner shop, complete with olive tree and information. **BELOW:** The vegetarian counter features green tiles in various shades of green.

Eataly
New York

Costa Group *Riccò del Golfo, La Spezia, Italy*
TPG Architecture *New York*

Eataly is located in New York City's historic Toy Building.

Eataly is a sprawling, 4,180 m2 artisanal Italian food and wine marketplace that recently opened in New York City's Flatiron District. It's the brainchild of Oscar Farinetti, who founded the concept in Turin, Italy, and chefs Mario Batali, Lidia Bastianich and Joe Bastianich of the Batali and Bastianich Hospitality Group. TPG Architecture was the architect for the complex and unique store fronts and interior, and Italy's Costa Group was responsible for the fittings and fixtures.

The concept behind Eataly, both in New York and its other locations in Italy and Japan, is to combine a marketplace that offers a vast selection of Italian delicacies — including cured and fresh meats, cheeses, fruits and vegetables, seafood, handmade pasta, gelato, desserts, bread and baked goods, coffee and wine — with eateries, cafes and restaurants of various sizes and styles — all under one roof. In New York there's also a culinary educational center and, on the roof, a beer garden with its own craft brews. A real *cucina Italiana* experience.

Many of the retail areas are paired with dedicated eateries, including the most formal restaurant in the space, *Manzo*, which celebrates meat, and *La Piazza,* a cheese and salami counter featuring marble-countered bars and standing tables. Elsewhere, bread is baked in a traditional wood-fire oven and a wine bar serves food gathered from the surrounding departments. There is also a separate wine shop with its own entrance (to comply with New York State liquor laws), and a pizza counter with direct access to the street for quick pickup.

For these many functions Costa Group created and refined fixtures to both reflect the products and meet American retailing needs. For the vegetarian restaurant, *Le Verdure,* which offers dishes prepared from local produce, the designers looked to the colors of nature for inspiration. The fish department and its accompanying seafood restaurant, *Il Pesce*, are styled after an Italian fishing village.

Eataly, New York, by its sheer size and depth of quality product offering, is fast becoming the city's ultimate destination for food lovers.

The vast space encompasses many individual market stalls, providing customers with intimate spaces in which to peruse the products and personal service to help with their selections.

Customers can choose from a wide assortment of restaurants and eateries from cafes and counters to restaurants with full wait service.

The selection available at Eataly is enormous, from cheeses and meats to breads and coffee, it's a panorama of all things Italian and delicious.

FIXTURE DESIGN: **Costa Group,** Riccò del Golfo, La Spezia, Italy

ARCHITECTURE: **TPG Architecture,** New York, NY

STORE SIZE: **4,180 m2,** (45,000 sq. ft.)

PHOTOGRAPHY: ©**Costagroup.net**
Alec Zaballero, TPG Architecture, New York, NY

Edward Marc Chocolatier

The Pentagon, Washington, D.C.

Design Republica
Washington, D.C.

The chocolates are arranged on a custom-built Carrera Marble counter backed by a large wood-framed mirror and accented with butterscotch-toned pendants.

Edward Marc Chocolatier is a family owned and operated gourmet chocolate and confectionery company founded in 1914 with a single store in Pittsburgh Pennsylvania. Despite the recent economic uncertainty, the family decided that, after 96 years, it was finally time to expand the brand and embark on a new, national marketing program. The first expansion location, shown here, is within the Pentagon building in Washington D.C.

The owners tasked Design Republica with the design and asked that the store reflect the vintage feel of their family-run business while incorporating their new, modern branding ideas. Even though the space is small the retailer's needs included an area to make chocolates and fudge bars and enough room for viewing and selecting chocolates, candy and merchandise throughout the space.

Francisco Beltran, AIA, Principal at Design Republica says, "*We immediately recognized that the exquisite gourmet chocolates should be the focal point for the store. We arranged and placed the chocolates on a custom-built Carrera Marble counter backed by a large wood-framed mirror and accented with butterscotch-toned pendants to attract a customer's attention upon entering the shop. The chocolate and fudge making area was placed along the storefront window to provide passersby a glimpse of what was being freshly prepared. The candy area provided a colorful anchor to the other end of the store. In this way, we maximized merchandising and storage space and created distinct areas for each aspect of the store's services.*"

By virtue of its confectionery-inspired theme, the shop's interior is a collection of rich dark chocolates, glistening caramels, soft crèmes and nougats, and warm citrus accents. The designers wanted to

The warm colors of the design complement the cool blue of Edward Marc's signature blue packaging.

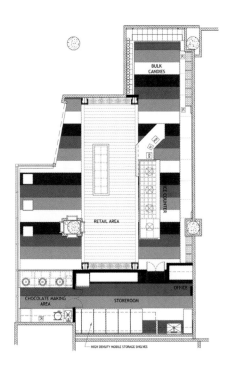

DESIGN: **Design Republica, Inc.,** Washington, D.C.

PROJECT TEAM: **Francisco A. Beltran, AIA; Jeanne M. Jarvaise**

STORE SIZE: **102 m2 (**1,100 sq. ft.)

PHOTOGRAPHY: **Ken Willis**

Sepia-toned, historical images of candy making decorate the shop.

create a space that delivered a luxurious old-world atmosphere through the use of traditional materials such as white marble, dark woods, custom metallic foiled wall treatments, and sepia toned murals. Beautifully contrasting with this warm, dark color palette is Edward Marc's signature blue color, found on the packaging.

Christian Edwards, proprietor, sums up the project, *"The design of the store more than met our expectations both operationally and aesthetically. To have every detail taken into consideration in the design has directly impacted the success of the store and the growth of our business."*

Gold Gourmet

Porto Arabia, The Pearl, Qatar

Part of ABU ISSA HOLDING
Doha-Qatar

Gold Gourmet is a new concept chocolatier in Qatar that offers gourmet chocolate and confectionery products from the finest brands in the world. Available at the shop are Maxim De Paris, a French brand known worldwide for its high quality, and an exclusive selection from the Swiss brand, Goldkenn. This brand's innovative and diverse packaging make it especially attractive for gift purchases. Also available at the new shop are the famous Turkish delights and flavors from Divan. The goal of Gold Gourmet is to project the high quality of its merchandise and evolve customer expectations to a new level.

The brands are prominently displayed around the perimeter of the shop, each in its own dark brown display unit with clear shelving and glass backing boards painted brown — allowing the products themselves to shine. Acrylic signage on stainless steel brackets at the top of each unit labels the brand.

The centerpiece of the store is the cash/wrap counter, placed in a central location and clad in gold. Behind it a wall of Bisazza mosaic tiles displays the store logo in gold finish, while suspended above are elegant, gold-finished pendant lights.

Tables of varying heights in gold-plated aluminum with mirrored tops serve as mid-floor displays and to one side of the shop, chocolate-brown chairs surround a gold-finished coffee table. Inviting customers to peruse the products in a relaxed manner.

The entire space is framed from above by a dark wood, trellis ceiling structure, and from below by white Kirari marble flooring. Hanging black-finished lights are interspersed in the ceiling trellis and the surrounding white perimeter holds white-finished recessed lighting.

On the facade gold-plated lettering in Arabic and English is illuminated with LED lighting to create a glowing effect on the chocolate-brown bulkhead.

DESIGN: **Zebra Projects FZE**
FIXTURES: **United Falcon**
STORE SIZE: **67 m2** (721 sq. ft.)

ABOVE: The brands are showcased in display units that line the perimeter of the space. BELOW: Within the small store the designers have created smaller, more intimate areas for customers to relax and examine the merchandise.

Napa Farms Market

San Francisco Airport Terminal 2, San Francisco

BALDAUF CATTON VON ECKARTSBERG Architects

San Francisco

Napa Farms Market's elegant presence along airport passage hints at the variety and quality of goods within the Market. The expansive, panoramic entry opens beneath a low-slung header clad in horizontal terra cotta planks.

Napa Farms Market is a market and retail store located in San Francisco International Airport's newly renovated Terminal 2 and stocked with foods from Bay Area artisanal food producers. It's the first airport dining program in the country to recruit food vendors that offer locally-sourced and wholesome fare prepared in a healthy manner.

Food merchants and producers from Northern California such as Tyler Florence, Equator Coffee, Vino Volo, Acme Bread, Cowgirl Creamery, Kara's Cupcakes and Three Twins ice cream are featured at discrete locations within the Market, combining the bounty of a farmers' market with the convenience of prepared foods.

Napa Farms Market was conceived and developed by BALDAUF CATTON VON ECKARTSBERG Architects, one of the key players in the development of two of the Bay Area's iconic food meccas — San Francisco's Ferry Building Marketplace and Napa's Oxbow Public Market. Utilizing its experience with these markets, BCV combined and transformed the elements found in successful market halls into a viable, single-space retail concept for an airport location — a concept ultimately captured in the project's tag line, "Farm to Flight."

Chris von Eckartsberg of BCV states, *"This packed and plentiful store was conceived as a microcosm of the larger market halls for which BCV is renowned. However, unlike these civic markets — typically housing collections of distinct and separate shops — Napa Farms makes use of an efficient, open single-room space, marked by a strikingly singular, modern market aesthetic. Sub-vendor branding is accomplished by elegant product displays and vendor signage."*

The design combines the classic feel of a traditional market — white beveled tile and Carrara marble floors and counters — with the rich warmth of more organic materials such as elm wood planking and shelving, natural cork ceiling and butcher block fixture tops. The palette of quality "real" materials, textures and tones are all appropriate for both the market concept and the high-traffic retail location.

"The contemporary design aesthetic for Napa Farms Market springs from a simple juxtaposition of complements of materials — warm against cool, industrial against organic," says von Eckartsberg, *"The overarching architectural statement and palette of Napa Farms Market celebrates the synergy of these opposites."*

TOP AND ABOVE LEFT: The Equator Coffee counter is front and center at the entrance and allows queuing into the terminal and views through to the rest of the Market space. **ABOVE RIGHT:** On the Fly offers easily accessed and cleanly displayed grab and go items.

ABOVE AND BELOW LEFT: The Acme Bread counter, with bread, cheese and pastry items, is the secondary central island station within the space. The look is contemporary but inviting with warm wood product displays, cork ceiling, and modern signage. BELOW RIGHT: The Vino Volo wine and packaged goods displays offer a variety of goods that encourages longer lingering.

At the rear of the space the Tyler Florence Rotisserie exhibition cookline serves made-to-order food and is the focal backdrop to the store. A common seating area is placed close by, offering a comfortable place to sit, distinct from the terminal.

BCV created both a strong, overarching aesthetic for the Napa Farms Market and also provided a strategy for individual vendor expression within the market.

DESIGN: **BALDAUF CATTON VON ECKARTSBERG Architects,** San Francisco, CA

CONTRACTOR: **Terra Nova,** Walnut Creek, CA

STORE SIZE: **371.5 m2** (4,000 sq. ft.)

PHOTOGRAPHER: **Rien van Rijthoven Architecture Photography**

Swiss Farms

Milmont Park, Pennsylvania

Chute Gerdeman

Columbus, Ohio

The pylon LED signs add visibility from the street, as does the hand-painted graphic mural on the façade and the silo.

DESIGN: **Chute Gerdeman,** Columbus, OH

PRINCIPAL: **Dennis Gerdeman**

PROGRAM DIRECTOR: **Andy McCoy**

VP BRAND COMMUNICATION: **Adam Limbach**

DIRECTOR OF ENVIRONMENTS: **Lynn Rosenbaum**

ARCHITECT/DESIGN DEVELOPMENT: **David Birnbaum**

SENIOR DESIGNER BRAND
COMMUNICATIONS: **Corey Dehus**

TREND & MATERIALS SPECIALIST: **Katie Clements**

PHOTOGRAPHY: **Brandon L. Jones Photography**

The usual greeting of "come on in" is replaced with "drive on in" at the Swiss Farms dairy chain. With plans to expand from a traditional quick dairy-purchase stop to one that offers pick-up dining options, Swiss Farms tasked Chute Gerdeman, with a complete brand transformation, including the new drive-through shop.

According to Chute Gerdeman, *"A new identity was designed to signal Swiss Farm's product shift, which expanded to include fresh produce, baked goods and prepared meals. The new identity creates a 'fresh from the farm' feel with the iconic rooster, sunrise imagery, and the new color palette. The curved horizon line gives the feeling of a landscape, and also speaks to the speed of the shopping process. The new design successfully communicates 'fresh express' to customers at a quick glance."* In addition to researching the practice, the service, the queuing process and the business as a whole, Chute Gerdeman provided the architecture, environmental design, brand communication, visual merchandising and graphic produc-

tion for this project. This is the new "Fresh Express" brand and the basis of the new design.

The new exterior includes elements from European barn architecture combined with a sleek shape, lots of glass and metal accents. The result is an architectural icon that not only attracts attention, but also quickly communicates Swiss Farm's unique service. *"The barn motif has been ramped up a few notches — complete with hand painted silo to create an eye-catching, all-American appeal."*

The 46-inch screens inside the glass-enclosed shop communicate the product offering to the customers in their cars. The interior is arranged to suggest a farmer's market with products displayed at the seated, driver's eye level. Making this concept effective are good visual merchandising and product display. TV monitors with technology that links the store to a meteorological website displays not only the weather/driving conditions but products appropriate for that time of the day.

wine shops

Aisle 43

St. Catharine's, Ontario

Perennial
Toronto

DESIGN: **Perennial, Toronto, ON**

DIRECTOR OF DESIGN, ENVIRONMENTS: **Tara O'Neil**

DIRECTOR OF COMMUNICATIONS: **Kelley Doris**

CREATIVE DIRECTOR: **Solange Rivard**

PHOTOGRAPHY: **Courtesy of Perennial**

Perennial, a Toronto-based design firm has built an enviable reputation for designing wine and grocery retail spaces. Working in close conjunction with personnel from the Andrew Peller Ltd. Group, the designers have unveiled a free-standing Aisle 43 store in Niagara's largest retail destination and with it they have launched *"a revolutionary way to discover and shop for Ontario wines."* The name — Aisle 43 — is a nod to the store's unique origins: *"those who know a bit about wine will be in on the secret right away; others will learn where it came from as soon as they venture in."*

Tara O'Neil, Director of Design, Environments, says that since the majority of Aisle 43 shops are located in, and part of, grocery stores, *"every detail of the store, right down to the fixtures, was specifically chosen to reflect the fact that Aisle 43 is a natural extension of the grocery store experience."*

The colors are bright, strong with vibrant reds and yellows floating in a white space and easy-to-navigate categories. The design includes Ontario's first retail automatic wine tasting unit that *"entices, enlivens and educates"* shoppers. For one dollar consumers can taste from a selection of wines

through this automatic dispenser and the dollar will be refunded upon purchase of a bottle of wine.

Colors and icons are used together with *"personality profiles"* rather than the traditional industry jargon often used in wine stores. Products are organized by the way people usually select their wines — red or white — then by price rather than by country or varietal way-finding systems. According to Kelley Doris, Director of Communications at Perennial, *"Our goal was to design a retail space and create an in-store language that democratizes wine and enhances the consumer's sense of fun and discovery."*

Solange Rivard, Creative Director, adds, *"We also wanted to take advantage of the great front-line staff, to provide a theater-like atmosphere where they can demonstrate their expertise and pride in the Andrew Peller Ltd. Wines."*

A.M. Wine Shoppe

Adams Morgan, Washington, D.C.

Design Republica
Washington, D.C.

A.M. Wine Shoppe is a extension of Justin Abad's restaurant, Cashion's Eat Place in Washington, D.C. The concept for the store, designed by Design Republica, was to offer the same select specialty wines featured in the restaurant to consumers in the surrounding Adams Morgan neighborhood.

Unlike most wine stores in which every inch of space is filled with shelves and bottles, A.M. Wine Shoppe provides a relaxed and uncluttered space for customers to peruse and sample the wines and accompanying charcuterie and cheese offerings.

The raw space the designers had to work with was grim — a small, dark basement with poor lighting and no presence on vibrant 18th Street, the commercial hub of the neighborhood. A limited budget meant the firm needed to be creative in the selection and use of finishes and materials.

Francisco Beltran, AIA, Principal at Design Republica details the design decisions, *"We introduced low voltage lighting to illuminate the mer-*

chandise and decorative halogen fixtures centered over the tasting table. The custom, 16-foot wood tasting table was centered in the space and is used for formal wine tastings and seminars while allowing a natural flow of movement. Custom faux timber shelves line the feature wall and provide an easily accessible and organized wine display. At the rear of the store we placed the work area and deli display showcasing charcuterie and cheeses. The original terrazzo and mosaic floor tiles were in good condition, so we elected to repair tiles where needed and polish the floor for a finished look. Certified Paldao wood wall covering was used to soften the walls and create a warm interior reminiscent of a traditional wine caskets."

Abad reports that, since opening, A.M. Wine Shoppe has outperformed revenue projections and the central tasting table has become the heart of the store — and the street — a place where customers and wine experts gather to discuss wine, food and happenings in the neighborhood.

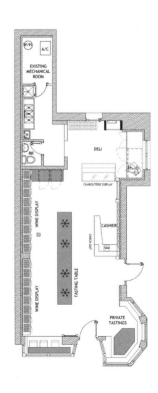

DESIGN: **Design Republica, Inc.,** Washington, D.C.

PROJECT TEAM: **Francisco A. Beltran, AIA; Jeanne M. Jarvaise**

STORE SIZE: **77 m2** (830 sq. ft.)

PHOTOGRAPHY: **Ken Willis**

Customers gather around the central display table to taste wine and the accompanying charcuterie and cheese offerings. Wood-framed chalkboards list the specials of the day.

El Mundo del Vino

Isidora 3000 Building, Las Condes, Santiago, Chile

Droguett A&A Ltda
Estudio Echeverría Edwards & Cía Ltda
Santiago, Chile

Graphics panels in the Isidora Goyenechea Street windows after hours. Ingeniously, a fourth panel under the wine glass panel, appears at closing time, when each panel slides over, closing the open areas that reveal the interior spaces during store hours. This view is at bottom of floor plan, below.

El Mundo del Vino is the largest wine retailer and distributor in Chile and one of the largest in South America.

This new flagship store for El Mundo del Vino is located within in the Las Condes district, one of the most elegant and refined areas of Santiago, Chile. The store is in the Isidora 3000 building which houses the W Hotel from the fourth floor upward, and stores, restaurants, and a fitness center from underground to the third floor.

The directive from corporate management was to *"create the best wine store in the world."* Tony Chi and

Associates, New York City, the designer of the W Hotel, was commissioned to strengthen the design and image synergies between the El Mundo del Vino and the W hotel. To that end, Droguett A&A and Estudio Echeverría Edwards were selected as co-architects and designers. Tony Chi developed the main lines, direction, and overall vision. Echeverría Edwards focused on design, decoration and materials, and Droguett A&A's main thrust on the project was furniture and construction solutions.

As Freddy Droguett elaborated, *"Utilizing our experience working with El Mundo del Vino for more*

ABOVE: Walls created by the back sides of the towering chambers are covered on one side with large purple-colored photographs of grapes, wine glasses, and bottle seals. Facing them across the plaza are green-colored images of vines, grape clusters, and wine-filled glasses. View from the front of the store toward mezzanine and red leather doors of fine wines cellar.

RIGHT: Depth is visually elongated by the separation created between cabinets using golden wood floors and laminated ceiling boxes of similar color wood texture to connect opposing units. Each box is punctuated with a deep rectangular trough of triple-bulb, recessed lighting in proportion to the box. Alternating with the wood, light gray floor tile with wine-red ceilings open passage spaces between cabinets (playing to the natural curiosity to peek through), producing a slower, browsing shopping pace. View from the mezzanine to Isidora Goyenechea Street door.

than ten years, and coupled with my own personal knowledge in wine tasting and the Chilean wine market, we were tasked with creating a unique place, elegant and trendy, but also with a festive approach. In other words, transform wine shopping into a more casual and exciting experience.

"Initially, we recognized the need to create, on one hand, a sense of unity within a space having dual access (one from the street, the second from the building atrium) and two floor levels; while on the other hand, give a sense of diversity for the varied products exhibited. To differentiate customer flow and movement through the store, three main spaces were designed: the upper level or mezzanine, the main plaza, and the chambers hallways on the lower level."

Approaching the store, the main windows utilize giant floor-to-ceiling photo murals on movable panels. "We thought it better for a commercial facade to have these panels facing the street, replacing what would be a large dark space after hours. They allow the store to present 'wine' to the public, even while the store is closed," Droguett explained.

Color is one of the most important design elements: the various floor, ceiling, and wall treat-

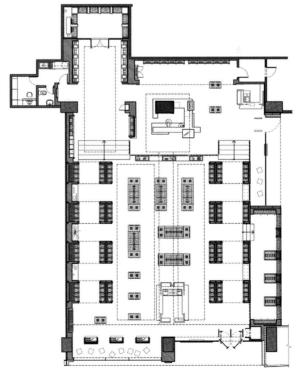

Floor plan of first floor, showing street façade entrance and windows at the bottom; the chambers hallways on either side of main plaza; mezzanine with displays for liquors, champagnes, sparkling wines; the premium wines cellar, the wine tasting counter and atrium entrance at the top.

RIGHT AND BELOW RIGHT: Champagne and sparkling wines are presented in a large wine-bottle deep display unit of dark wood, framed with brushed metal, that seems to float from the highly polished stainless steel wall it nearly covers. Set deep within the expanse of dark cedar are precisely random, recessed illuminated display cases lined in high-gloss brass in which premium bottles are showcased. Warm tones of metal and wood and flooring, all combine to create the golden aura of champagne. Lush padded red leather doors herald the special room within.

BELOW LEFT: The integrated aromas of cedar, cellar, and leather, associated with expensive wine cellars, fill the temperature-controlled air.

ABOVE RIGHT AND LEFT: A light box for wines and glasses to rest on gives depth and life to the wines being tasted at the counter on the mezzanine. The area, overlooking the plaza's wine-themed graphics and glimpses into the chambers halls, is set off by mirror-polished stainless steel on the cabinet faces, dark cedar walls and counter tops with steel trim moldings, and the textured stainless steel ceilings. BELOW: Accessories area. Backlit cases with glass shelves create glowing focus to featured displays. Cases on left back the sliding panels of the Isidora Goyenechea Street windows. The ladder provides access to the topmost wine cubbies.

DESIGN: **Droguett A&A Ltda,** Santiago, Chile
Estudio Echeverria Edwards & Cía Ltda. Santiago, Chile

ARCHITECT DIRECTOR:
Freddy Droguett H.

PROJECT DESIGNER:
Roberto Pertuz D.

ARCHITECT DIRECTOR:
Sergio Echeverría

PROJECT DESIGNERS:
Miguel Dulanto / Pablo Lamarca / Rodrigo Castillo

GENERAL CONTRACTOR:
Alex Zóffoli, Constructora Zoff

DESIGN CONSULTANT: **Toni Chi & Associates,** New York, NY

STORE MANAGER:
Humberto Cuevas

PHOTOGRAPHER:
Marcos Mendizábal

ments make it a delightful, visually stimulating experience, beginning with either of the two entry ways. Integral to the design, colors run from the red of the corporate identity on the entry, to bright yellow and red on display units, to light and medium gray ceramic floor tiles, golden wood flooring segments, light gray painted ceiling areas, ultra dark brown stained cedar wood, to stainless steel in polished silver or golden textured finishes.

Bright red lattice work entry and doors present a graphic image of wine racks. The doors, with custom-sculpted stainless steel door handles shaped like giant corkscrews, visually alert shoppers they are about to enter a store that is anything but ordinary.

The mezzanine, accessed by a dual-toned, ceramic-tiled stairway, offers immense diversity in product display along with an elegant wine tasting area. The *pièce de résistance* wine cellar at the far end of the mezzanine is announced by luxurious padded red leather entry doors with striking square brass handles that open on a display room envelop-

ed in natural cedar from the louvered ceiling to the cabinet trim.

The plaza area, surrounded by the chambers, is a dramatic open space, and even more use of color and light enhances consumers' sense of openness and freedom of movement. The main plaza exhibits wines in low display units constructed of dark cedar frames with yellow- and red-painted cubbies and tops.

The chambers, appearing as a series of connected — yet separate — rooms sided by dark cedar, are actually floor-to-ceiling display units flanking the main plaza's waist-high display racks. Walking through the long chambers formed by grids of golden cedar cubbies, customers can peek into the plaza areas after strolling past each chamber's fully-stocked cabinets.

Carrying through the rich, dark brown cedar theme on both the mezzanine and plaza, elegant cash and wrap counters complete the experience of shopping in "the best wine store in the world."

BELOW: Dark brown walls, gray floor tiles, and golden wood laminate ceilings, frame views of the distilled spirits and wine tasting sections of the mezzanine. Side illumination of the spirits displayed on glass shelves create a bright, inviting, and festive mood that reflects their colors on the textured metal ceilings. The cash-wrap counter faces the building's atrium entrance.

Gary's Wine & Marketplace

Wayne, New Jersey

Tricarico Architecture & Design

Wayne, New Jersey

The space is vast — 2,230 m2 and ceilings are 6.7 m high — however, the client, Gary Fisch, had a vision that was even bigger than this space. The challenge for the architects and designers at Tricarico Architecture & Design was to incorporate the client's requirements, understand his philosophy on how he operates a store and speak to the customers through visuals and the overall excitement and the experiences they will have in the space.

What was Gary's vision? *"Picture yourself traveling through Europe and you come across a quaint village and discover a spectacular courtyard filled with fresh foods and wine. As you enter the courtyard you come across artisans making baskets with wonderful gourmet foods and bottles of wine in them. To your left you are swept away by the sweet smells of orchids and roses at the local flower shop. The florist's shop is beneath a Tuscan home of stucco, architectural quoins and a clay tile roof. The center of the courtyard is flanked by trees, benches and street lanterns."* Get the picture?

The problem: making the space feel *"comfortable and personal"* for the shopper and making this setting different from what other wine retailers are doing. The designers also had to include two coolers; one for wines and another for beer and champagne. The client wanted manager and security offices to overlook the space. To solve that problem a mezzanine was constructed that not only maximized the space but made the store look less like a supermarket. The mezzanine now serves as the portal or entry into the store proper and the main floor action can be viewed through the residential style windows of a stucco Tuscan house that is part of the theater of the total design.

In addition to the wine and beers in the coolers, the designers had to plan 112 feet of wall space for the non-cooled beers, 425 feet for the wines from around the world and another 80 feet for spirits. Zones were also created for gourmet foods, prep areas, the deli counter, a flower shop and a basket filling areas. There are also 12 check out counters.

The existing concrete floor was polished and the walls were finished with a crème color and a stone wainscot. *"The palette has an old world European feel with influences of yellow, orange, green and violet. It had to work with the merchandise and not compete with the vast array of colors on labels or any of the gourmet packaging."* This was accomplished by having the gondolas

and the fixtures neutral in color and using splashes of the colors previously mentioned for the end caps and the displays.

All glass cases are lit and recessed into the walls except the cases in the deli area. Custom gondolas, lower in height, were created for the wines. Visual merchandising plays an important role in the overall scheme and the table tops and end caps serve to bring featured merchandise into prominence.

In a space of this size signage and graphics are vital. *"It was key to place the graphics and signage at the right eye level and location."* Overhead signs were used to identify areas, products or services and in the deli area there are awnings over the cases that carry the product identification. In the wine area, the bottles are identified by the countries from

which they were imported. At the rear of the store, large windows set high up on the wall also have awnings and here they read Beer, Wine, Champagne, Saki, etc. *"All signage awnings have a weathered look as if they have been there for decades."*

To illuminate the store, the track and pendant lights were brought down to 9.5 feet off the floor. *"This was done to bring the lighting to a level that is comfortable for the customer"* and to highlight the displays. Gold reflectors over the track lights *"create the feeling of warmth and a more natural light."* Street lanterns were placed throughout and when the cash station is open — the lantern light near it is on. Visions do come true.

DESIGN: **Tricarico Architecture & Design,** Wayne, NJ

SENIOR PROJECT MANAGER: **TNiko Verikios**

PROJECT MANAGER: **Pallavi Padgilwar**

CONSTRUCTION PROJECT MANAGER: **Antonio Spina**

ASST. PROJECT MANAGER: **Cara Rossomando**

INTERIOR DESIGNERS: **Joanna Pobicki, Nicole Tricarico**

PHOTOGRAPHY: **Sean O'Brien Photography,** Pompton Lakes, NJ

Marques de Riscal

Elciego, Alava, Spain

MARKETING-JAZZ
Madrid

When Marques de Riscal, one of the most traditional wineries in Spain, needed to redesign their on-site shop they approached Carlos Aires of MARKETING-JAZZ with the project. When the management of the shop first met with Aires they had two main concerns: They wanted to sell branded merchandise in addition to the fine wines they already produced and sold, and with the re-design of the space, they wanted to be as "green" and economical as possible. This meant using existing furniture and doing as little construction work as possible.

The owners firmly believed that Marques de Riscal was not just a winery, but a lifestyle brand. This had to be reflected in the merchandise mix of the shop. To display the branded items such as t-shirts and other articles of clothing, Aires and his team closed in windows on the left-hand of the shop to create "closets." The resulting alcoves would serve to display the branded items singly with appropriate backdrops that included photographs of the landmark winery.

To improve the wine buying experience and encourage impulse buying, display tables were placed to allow casual and easy circulation around them and the cash/wrap was moved to the back of the space to lessen the "sales" pressure from the staff and allow customers to browse at their leisure.

Without hindering the casual shopping experience, the owners also needed to promote the idea of their wines as one of the finer things —

TOP: One of the ornate display cases. RIGHT: The overall atmosphere of the store retails the atmosphere of a traditional winery with stone walls, exposed rafters and vaulted wood ceiling.

one of life's little luxuries. To achieve this the central display area was raised a few inches off the ground and lighting tubes were placed around the perimeter of the raised platform. This gives the impression of the wine being in an exultant position, almost on an alter. In keeping with the economic directive, these walkways and display tables were placed to allow the use of existing lighting.

On the right-hand wall original shelving was lined with custom panels and utilized to showcase the winery's very best wines as well as promote self-service. On this wall in-set display boxes are mixed with tradition wine-hold niches that form a diamond shape.

The various displays, in combination with the stone walls, exposed wooden beams and vaulted ceiling of the original space, give customers the impression of being in a very special place and brands the wine and other merchandise as items necessary to a appealing lifestyle — within everyone's reach.

DESIGN: **MARKETING-JAZZ,** Madrid

CREATIVE DIRECTOR AND FURNITURE DESIGN: **Carlos Aires**

ILLUSTRATION AND SKETCHES: **Elena de Andres**

PHOTOGRAPHER: **Luis Sanchez de Pedro Aires**

Stratus Winery

Niagara-on-the-Lake, Ontario

burdifilek
Toronto

Cutting a dramatic profile amid the numerous vineyards and wineries in Niagara-on-the-Lake, is the modern structure designed by burdifilek for Stratus Wines. Burdifilek was commissioned to "create an atmosphere that is an extension of Stratus' unconventional approach to winemaking and which would complement the distinct surrounding landscape."

Contained in the structure are a combined retail and tasting area and two private tasting rooms, all exposed to the surrounding natural setting through 20-foot windows. Light floods the interior and the site lines were designed to allow the outside landscape to always form the backdrop.

Diego Burdi, creative partner at burdifilek explains, *"We wanted to make a strong sculptural statement within the beautiful volume of space. There was a reflective quality to the rich, charcoal terrazzo floor that we wanted to take advantage of, so we created a library of wine around the perimeter of the space, and in the center, a dramatic sculptural box to compartmentalize a smaller display area."* The outside of this box is a series of undulating vertical sand-blasted and rift-cut oak forms which are encased in a blackened steel surround. Inside, bottles fill the structure from floor to ceiling. *"The design makes the solid mass seem light and creates the visual illusion of gentle movement."*

Serving as the main wine tasting bar is an uninterrupted slab of white marble resting atop a base of white-washed oak. Behind the bar full-height shelves flank a painting by Richard Halliday. Through floor-to-ceiling windows and the moveable black mahogany decorative screens, visitors are treated to a view of the production floor.

Two smaller tasting rooms create more intimate settings. In one, a hand-finished, dove-gray wall meets a sculptural Paralam ceiling, with the wine production floor becoming *"an architectural feature through the creation of a transparent wall and illuminated wine barrels."* The second tasting room is even more secluded — here the walls are lined in copper-rust toned squares of end-cut, oiled mesquite wood. Wooden louvers control the light, and two large ebony colored lighting fixtures *"reference the theme of oversized scale and proportion."*

ABOVE: Inside the central sculptural box, wine is diplay in floor-to-ceiling shelving. BELOW: Two small, private tasting rooms create intimate settings.

DESIGN: **burdifilek,**
Toronto, ON, Canada

CREATIVE PARTNER: **Diego Burdi**

MANAGING PARTNER: **Paul Filek**

SENIOR DESIGNERS:
**Jeremy Mendenca,
Young Sak-Kim**

SENIOR CAD TECHNICIANS:
Mauro Lobo-Pires, Tracy Morton

DESIGNERS: **Mariko Nakagawa,
Alsion Priestman, Willow Lau**

CLIENT TEAM: **Stephen Cohen,
Carol Marotta**

PHOTOGRAPHY: **BenRahn,
A-Frame Inc.**

Winestore
Charlotte, North Carolina

Core Architecture + Design
Washington, D.C.

According to the design team at Core Architecture & Design the objective was *"to develop a contemporary, user-friendly wine specialty retail prototype,"* including custom fixtures, graphics and displays for the Winestore. *"The architecture and interior design was carefully coordinated with the branding and identity package to create a concept that embodied a fresh, clean and accessible approach to learning about, appreciating and finding the perfect bottle of wine."*

Bold colors, vibrant graphics and a traffic flow that encourages shoppers to explore — to discover — set the look for the space. *"The design reflects ease of merchandising, colorful and accessible product information and custom fixtures that can quickly change products and marketing graphics."*

There are numerous interactive fixtures on the floor as well as product tasting devices integrated into some of the fixtures. Bottles are stored on the walls behind translucent sliding panels which makes it easier for shoppers to select wine and for the staff to replenish the stock.

Unique to this design concept are rotating product fixtures that are mounted floor to ceiling, each containing a group of wines. These fixtures offer wines grouped for occasion and/or pricing with labels such as: "First Date," "Dinner Party," "Girl's Night Out" — *"following the typical buying habits of most people who enter a wine store with a particular occasion or price point in mind."*

These fixtures are light looking, semi-transparent and easily changed to carry a new promotional story and stock. The signature "Winestore" red dot highlights each unit and carries the story.

White, satin finished steel, frosted acrylic and high gloss, steel-gray floors are the background for the accent colors — broad slashes of red and greenish yellow. They not only enliven the fascia over the wall-stocked bottles but classify the stock as to "red" or "white."

"From branding to graphics that encourage browsing to the clean layout, an ideal, non-threatening shopping experience infuses customers with confidence in their wine purchases."

DESIGN: **Core Architecture + Design,** Washington, D.C.

DESIGN PRINCIPAL: **Peter Hapstak, AIA, IIDA, ISP**

PROJECT PRINCIPAL: **Dale A. Stewart, AIA**

PROJECT MANAGER: **Cassanara Cullison, AIA, LEED, AP**

SENIOR DESIGNER: **Kathleen Claire Ngiam**

PROJECT ARCHITECT: **Marek Woodard**

PHOTOGRAPHY: **Michael Moran,** New York, NY

designer profiles

Gold Gourmet

Arabesq

ABUISSA HOLDING

Blue Salon Bldg, 3rd Floor,
Suhaim Bin Hamad Street,
P.O. Box: 6255 Doha-Qatar
Phone: +974 444 66 111
Fax: +974 444 66 112
Email: info@abuissa.com

www.abuissa.com

An aspired vision and an inspired mission leading the way forward

An impeccable portfolio built over three decades of successive and successful achievement, ABU ISSA HOLDING emerges to be one of the top-notch leading business groups in the Middle East.

The Group is one of Qatar's most diversified and progressive businesses with a solid capacity controlling and operating market-leading companies across the GCC region in various sectors including retail, distribution, telecommunications, IT, Energy & Engineering, Investment, real estate and other market operations.

Headquartered in the State of Qatar, ABU ISSA Holding holds majority shares in more than 20 companies across the Middle East. Striving to continuously challenge itself to dynamically grow its businesses, both internally and through world class partnerships, Abu Issa Holding is poised to set the highest standards of excellence and governance in the region.

With an extensive scope of business activities and an effective and professional workforce of more than 2000 employees, ABU ISSA HOLDING (AIH) is considered today one of the renowned leading family groups in the Gulf region.

AIH embodies an inspired mission to lead business growth in Qatar & Middle East by setting success modules for consultancy, construction, engineering, energy, ICT, investment, retail, distribution, services and joint-venture developments & other market operations.

With a proactive vivid vision to maintain and sustain successful joint ventures to support the overall economic development & GDP of The State of Qatar, AIH operates and provide a full range of innovative products and solutions to serve the emerging Qatari market and indulge in regional expansion through new concepts in the Middle East; who share globalization spirit and unique requirements.

Abu Issa Holding embraces the region's top retail activities, incorporating one of the largest international brand portfolios and enjoys customer confidence and delight. The vision of the management is evident in all its outlets and reflects effective planning, thought-process and futuristic-approach. The blend of brands and their positioning in Qatar's market portrays the strategic balance and vibrancy, which is a hallmark of Abu Issa Holding.

BALDAUF CATTON VON ECKARTSBERG Architects

1527 Stockton Street, 4th Floor
San Francisco, California, 94133
Phone: 415 398 6538
Fax: 415 398 6521
Email: info@bcvarch.com

www.bcvarch.com

Hog Island Oyster Bar

KEY PERSONNEL
Hans Baldauf, *Principal and CFO,* baldauf@bcvarch.com
Ken Catton, *Principal and CEO,* catton@bcvarch.com
Christian von Eckartsberg, *Principal and COO,* voneck@bcvarch.com

YEAR FOUNDED
1997

NUMBER OF EMPLOYEES
25

KEY CLIENTS
Retailers: California Academy of Sciences, Taste Partners, DLew Enterprises, Cowgirl Creamery, Sports Basement, Oxbow Market LLC, Williams-Sonoma Inc

Restaurants: Hog Island Oyster Co, Rodrich Management Group, Il Fornaio, Gott's Roadside, Moana Hotel and Restaurant Group

Wineries: Franciscan Estates Winery, Cakebread Winery, Viansa Winery

Hospitality: Shangri-La Hotels & Resorts, China World Hotel

Commercial Development: Brookfield Properties Corp, The Shorenstein Company, Madison Marquette, The Irvine Company Retail Properties, Wilson Meany Sullivan, Blake Hunt Ventures, J.S. Rosenfield & Company, Ellis Partners LLP

SERVICES OFFERED
Architecture, Master Planning, Interior Design, Furnishings, Graphic Design

Baldauf Catton von Eckartsberg Architects is a San Francisco based design firm known for the diversity of scales at which it works - from the master planning of large urban projects to the tableware used in our restaurant designs. The firm's principals pursue this range of work because they believe architecture and design are richest when they are informed by the breadth and complexity of human experience. An interest in the broad approach to a design problem lends itself to the multi-disciplinary character of BCV Architects and to experiences in urban design and planning, architecture, interiors, furnishing, and graphic design.

Baldauf Catton von Eckartsberg Architects' approach to sustainability is to examine the issue through multiple lenses – to not only seek engineering solutions but also to respond to the ethical, cultural, social, economic and historic implications of a project and its place in the environment. It is this approach that has informed projects such as San Francisco's Ferry Building Marketplace, Mercato in Bend, Oregon, the Oxbow Public Market in Napa, California and the new Master Plan for San Francisco's Treasure Island. In each of these, large conceptual ideas are refined and made meaningful by attention to the details of direct human interaction. BCV considers it essential to design projects that become vibrant communities and sustain the lives of their inhabitants and users.

SELECT AWARDS
2010
Great Places Award, American Planning Association – *Ferry Building Marketplace*
AIA|LA 6th Annual Restaurant Design Award - Bar/Lounge category Jury Award – *Press Club*
AIA SF Honor Award for Excellence in Interior Architecture – *Press Club*
Woodworks Interior Beauty of Wood Award – *Press Club*

2009
Honor Awards for Regional and Urban Design Focus on Mixed-Use Density – *Treasure Island Master Plan*

2008
AIA San Francisco: Special Achievement Award – *Slow Food Nation*
First Place Sit Down Restaurant, Retail Design Institute – *Anthology Supper Club*
First Place Specialty Food Shop, Retail Design Institute – *Press Club*

2007
EDRA/Places Design Award – *Ferry Building Marketplace*

2006
AIA San Francisco Design Award: Urban Design – *Treasure Island Master Plan*

2004
Preservation Design Award: Rehabilitation/Adaptive Reuse, California Preservation Foundation – *Ferry Building Marketplace*
Excellence in Design Award, AIA SF – *Ferry Building Marketplace*
Innovative Design and Construction of a New Project: Merit Certificate, ICSC Int'l Design & Development Awards – *Ferry Building Marketplace*

2003
San Francisco Architectural Heritage Award (Governor's Award), California Heritage Council – *Ferry Building Marketplace*
National Preservation Award, National Trust for Historic Preservation – *Ferry Building Marketplace*

2001
Best Retail Project Winner, San Francisco Business Times – *Olympia Place*

1999
Top Ten Great Hotel Restaurants in the World, Hotels Magazine – *Angelini Bangkok*

1998
International Store Interior Design, VM+SD – *Pottery Barn*

Virgin Atlantic Clubroom

Pava

Table 1280

Bergmeyer Associates, Inc.

51 Sleeper Street, 6th Floor
Boston, Massachusetts, 02210-1208
Phone: 617-542-1025
Fax: 617-542-1026
Email: marketing@bergmeyer.com

www.bergmeyer.com

KEY PERSONNEL
Michael R. Davis, *Principal*
Lewis Muhlfelder, Jr., *Principal*
Joseph P. Nevin, Jr., *Principal*
David Tubridy, *Principal*

KEY CLIENTS
TD Bank, Museum of Fine Arts-Boston, West Marine, Boloco, Lord & Taylor, Samsonite, Staples, Bassett, Cabela's, Cleveland Museum of Art, PUMA, Talbots

NEW CLIENT CONTACT
Anne Johnson

YEAR FOUNDED
1973

SERVICES OFFERED
Architecture, Interior Design, Space Planning, Programming, Merchandize Planning, Visual Merchandizing, Sustainable Design

Bergmeyer is a mid-sized architecture and interior design firm that designs for a broad range of human needs and experiences, from places where people live, work, and learn to destinations in retail and dining. Client engagement is central to our process. We facilitate regular conversations to get to know what matters most on the project, so that we can design environments that skillfully balance our clients' vision and aesthetic preferences with practical concerns for durability, functionality, budget, and schedule. We partner to help our clients perfect and excel at whatever they do through strategic, responsive, and elegant design solutions.

Collaboration is central to our process. In our office, teams work together in rooms specifically dedicated to their client's project and are supported by the latest technologies including Building Information Modeling. We share the BIM model with our consultants to enhance document quality and our in-house LEED Coordinator works with teams to find the most sustainable solutions for their projects resulting in LEED Certifications at all levels, including Platinum, for many of our clients' projects.

CIP Retail

9575 LeSaint Drive
Fairfield, Ohio 45014
Phone: 800-877-7373
Fax: 513-874-6246
Email: cip@cipstyle.com

www.CIPstyle.com

Ralph's Food Warehouse

Dave's Fresh Marketplace

YEAR FOUNDED
1975

NUMBER OF EMPLOYEES
90

SERVICES OFFERED
Creative Design, Engineering, Fabrication and Installation of interior décor components, signage and custom millwork

Founded in 1975, CIP is a leader in the design, manufacture, delivery and installation of retail environment solutions. Centrally located near Cincinnati in Fairfield, Ohio, CIP has national and global reach with a team of experienced design consultants.

CIP has earned a sterling reputation for service, meticulous attention to detail, and concern for its client's projects. Combined with a sprawling 120,000 square-foot state-of-the-art facility, CIP truly is in a class by itself. CIP's highly skilled designers, artisans, craftsmen and engineers work together seamlessly to deliver a level of quality that is second to none. At every stage, projects are given expert attention by specialists uniquely qualified in their discipline, each masters of their craft.

CREATIVE DESIGN
CIP is rooted in design. Whether it's developing an extension of an existing identity or creating a new concept from the ground up,

CIP's talented designers can help turn visions into reality or re-imagine a client's space in a totally new way. From supermarket design to small or large scale retail spaces, CIP can handle any challenge.

ENGINEERING
CIP has the technical know-how to translate beautiful design into functional elements customized for any space.

DECOR FABRICATION
Using the most effective methods and materials, CIP has the know-how to produce nearly anything a client can imagine and creates the finished product with an unmatched level of craftsmanship.

DELIVERY AND INSTALLATION
CIP sees projects through to the very end, with on-time delivery and professional installation.

PROJECT MANAGEMENT
CIP's turnkey approach ensures every job will be seamlessly handled by a single point of contact who knows the project inside and out, with constant attention given to budget, schedule and vision.

Body Café

Commercial Design Interiors, LLC

9121 Interline Ave, Suite 1B
Baton Rouge, Louisiana
Phone: 225-928-1190
Fax: 225-928-1199
Email: matthew@c-d-interiors.com

Licensed in Texas and Louisiana, servicing nationally

www.c-d-interiors.com

KEY PERSONNEL
Matthew Edmonds, LEED AP, ASID, IIDA
Co-Owner/Designer
Email: matthew@c-d-interiors.com

Tracy A. Burns ASID, IFMA
Co-Owner/ Designer, Woman-owned business
Email: tracy@c-d-interiors.com

KEY CLIENTS
Retail, Healthcare, Corporate, Restaurants/Bars, Sustainable

NEW CLIENT CONTACT
Matthew Edmonds

YEAR FOUNDED
2004

NUMBER OF EMPLOYEES
Five

AWARDS
2010 IIDA Awards
Award of Excellence – Hospitality, Hampton Inn & Suites
Award of Excellence – Retail, COX Communications Retail Center
Award of Excellence – Healthcare, Magnolia Assisted Living (Sustainable)
Award of Recognition – Government, Livingston Council Chambers

2010 South Central Chapter of ASID
Ovation Award Commercial– Hampton Inn & Suites
Gold Award – Hampton Inn & Suites
Silver Award – Magnolia Assisted Living (Sustainable)
Silver Award – Moto Rouge
Bronze Award – Livingston Parish Council Chambers

(Additional awards for previous years available at www.c-d-interiors.com)

Commercial Design Interiors, LLC offers commercial design experience with NCIDQ certificate holders and has registered interior designers with the State of Louisiana and Texas. The firm also has a LEED Accredited professional on staff to manage and facilitate LEED and sustainable projects.

Whether it is working, eating or shopping, the places Commercial Design Interiors, LLC creates are challenging and invigorating. The firm is less concerned with promoting a particular style and more about designing dynamic environments. Much of the work involves bringing new life to tired spaces; transforming an unproductive part of the built environment into a vibrant, integral part of the community. The firm's design process centers on a team approach to project development and delivery. Each team is responsible for a project throughout all phases of the design process. Commercial Design Interiors, LLC firmly believes the best designs result directly from dynamic collaboration between the clients and the designers.

In addition to using traditional methods of sketching, drafting and rendering, the designers make extensive use of the newest and most advanced technologies available for interior applications. This use of technology allows the firm to transfer and communicate electronic data, including drawings, to clients and consultants across the country and internationally.

Commercial Design Interiors, LLC have the experience, talent and desire to help make every client's vision of a project a reality.

Eataly, Genoa

Cioccolatitaliani

Eataly, New York

Costa Group

Via Valgraveglia Z.A.I.,
19020 Riccò del Golfo, Italy.
Phone/Fax: +39 0187 76 93 09/08
Email: info@costagroup.net

www.costagroup.net

KEY PERSONNEL
Franco Costa, Sandro Costa, *Co-owners*

KEY CLIENTS
Abades (E), Airest (E), Anema&Cozze (I), Areas (E) (Mex), Auchan/
SMA (I), Autogrill (I), B/E Ducasse Kaiser (F), Barilla (I), Blooming-
dale's (USA), Camst (D), Coop (I), Cremonini (I), Eataly New York/
Genova, Eat-out (E), Fauchon (F) (Marocco), Ferrero (I), Festival
Cinema Venezia (I), Fiat Auto (Japan) (I), Giovanni Rana (I) (GB),
Gruppo Ligresti (I), Gruppo Moncho's (E), Gruppo Sighor (F),
Heineken (E), HMS (D), La Fayette (F) (UAE), La Granda (I), La
Sure–a/100 Montadito (E), Lancia Auto (I), Lavazza (USA), Lizarran
(E) (F), Maison Kaiser (F), Mallorca (E), Mc Donald's (I), Obikˆ (I),
Panino Giusto (I), Parmacotto (USA), Pastificcio (E), Paul/Roy (F),
Princi (I), Rossopomodoro (I) (GB), Selfridges (GB), SPC Korea
(Korea), SSP Compass (D), Tartine Avenue (F), Technogym (I),
Torreblanca (E), Vergnano (USA), ecc.

Curiosity and vitality have always been the diving force behind
Costa Group, a company specializing in the Food Entertainment
business since the early eighties.

Growth has been steady: To date, the Costa Group has designed
more than 5000 shops worldwide and implements about 20
projects per month. The offices encompass 11,000 square meters
and the company operates several plants specializing in the
manufacture of wood, steel, marble, glass and fiberglass fixtures
and fittings. All production stages are integrated in order to supply
a "turn key" shop.

The company is owned by the brothers Franco and Sandro
Costa who continually strive to create an atmosphere that encourages creativity and welcomes risk — nurturing a creative process
that finds solutions to design challenges and paves the way for
innovation. The firm has more than 100 employees, acknowledged
by the owners as the firm's real capital.

The firm's philosophy is "to always play with food" and to work
with simple and good things, easy to mix and suitable for obtaining
top results. Starting from architecture, the firm creates 360 degrees
projects, where space is above all about communication.

One of the main features of the company is the total design and
realizations of shops in its headquarters — from the study of the
format, to simulation in their factory, to the shop installation and
the following assistance to the customer.

Their mission is "taking care of the customer BEFORE, DURING
AND AFTER," and they believe the most vital component to this
mission is communication. Everyday discussions take place not just
between architects and designers, but also communication experts
who contribute to the development of ideas.

To understand the needs of its clients, the Costa Group studies
the details of each new project — the location of the shop, the
products to be sold, the personality of the owner, and most
importantly the customer. Clients are fully participatory in the
process —active partners making informed choices and guided by
ecological and social concerns in addition to the practicalities of
their shops.

The Costa group wants its clients to understand that they are
not hiring a single designer, but a partner to delegate their needs,
to study the feasibility of a project, and to create materially the
client's dream and then assist him or her after the installation of the
shop.

This comprehensive service is what stands the Costa Group far
ahead of its competition and makes it possible for the firm to
experiment with, and develop shop formats that lead the industry.

A.M. Wine Shoppe

Edward Marc

Cafesa

design republica

1909 19th Street NW, Suite 404
Washington D.C.
Phone: 202-462-6762
Fax: 202-422-6763
Email: fbeltran@designrepublica.com

www.designrepublica.com

KEY PERSONNEL

Francisco A. Beltran, AIA, *Principal and Director of Design*
fbeltran@designrepublica.com

Jeanne M. Jarvaise, *Principal and Director of Interiors*
jjarvaise@designrepublica.com

KEY CLIENTS

Lebanese Taverna Restaurant Group, Sam and Harry's Restaurant Holdings, The Caucus Room LLC, Edward Marc Chocolatier, Magic Meals Restaurant Group, Occasions Caterers, Cashion's Restaurant Group, Hilton Hotels, Westin Hotels, Tash Restaurant, DC Crossfit

YEAR FOUNDED

2000

NUMBER OF EMPLOYEES

Five

SERVICES OFFERED

Design Republica, is a Washington DC based firm offering a comprehensive vision and approach to design — from architecture and interiors to communication design

design republica \di-ˈzīn\ \ri-ˈp əb-lik- ə\   n: a body of persons freely engaged in the creative art of executing aesthetically functional design. A collective of individuals formed to innovate, create and manifest with wild imagination, mad artistry, and a passion for detail.

HISTORY

Co-founded in 2000 by principals Francisco Beltran, AIA and Jeanne Jarvaise, Associate AIA, Design Republica's partners have over fifteen years of experience in architecture, interior design and business development. With a focus on efficient and inventive use of materials and space, Design Republica finds their passion and joy in the creation of beautifully streamlined restaurant, hospitality, office, and retail environs.

PHILOSOPHY

At Design Republica, they understand that space design is many things to many people. Some people think it means an efficient operating environment, some a beautiful interior, while others just a necessary part of any new retail business. To Design Republica, it's all of those things and more. Good space design is that intangible business asset that allows a client's customers to connect to their services, products and environment on an emotional level. Truly innovative space design attracts, inspires and creates desires, motivating consumers to respond positively to an environment or message, e.g., restaurant, store, office or product. Design Republica integrates brand identity, business concept, and operations into a cohesive targeted approach, ultimately making a positive impact on every client's bottom line.

El Mundo del Vino

Droguett A&A Ltda.

Padre Mariano 10, of. 306
Providencia, Santiago, Chile
Phone: 562 – 235 55 67
Fax: 562 – 235 17 53
Email: info@daa.cl — fd@daa.cl

www.daa.cl

KEY PERSONNEL

Freddy Droguett H. Architect, *Director*
Mauricio Muñoz Architect, *Supermarket division*
Ma. Antonieta Cepeda, *Architect, Fitness Centers and boutiques division*
Tomás González Architect, *Restaurant division*
Cristian Torres Architect, *Franchises division*
Cristian Espínola, *3D modelling and renders director*

KEY CLIENTS

Cencosud S.A., El Mundo del Vino, Sportlife, Grupo Areas, Privilege, Unifood, Nestlé, Caffarena

SERVICES OFFERED

Architecture, interior design, furniture design, lighting design

Droguett A&A was founded by Freddy Droguett H. in 1999 and is located in Santiago, the capital and largest city in Chile. From the firm's very first clients, which included El Mundo del Vino and Nestlé, to the current client roster which includes the biggest names in Chile, South America and the world, Droguett's goals have always centered on the commercial success of the finished project. The business objectives and needs of the client must be met — all else follows.

Throughout it's history Droguett and his firm have created branded spaces that faithfully represent the attributes and personality of each client's identity, and effectively communicate that identity to the end consumer — the shopper.

By using these two entities — the client and *their* client, the shopper — as sources of inspiration, the designers have been able to generate concepts and ideas that strengthen the bonds between store and consumer — between design firm and client. For many of Droguett's clients this collaboration has deepened and expanded through years of successful projects and venues. All of this produces measurable and verifiable results.

The firm naturally loves good design; however, it does not rely purely on inspiration or the blind reiteration of the newest trends. What Droguett and his team do is *listen*. They know how to hear, and empathize with, their clients, ensuring that all particulars of a project live up to, or exceed, expectations.

Everyone involved in a project participates in a systematic methodology that evaluates each element from every conceivable perspective. This systematic and team-centered strategy informs all design decisions and ensures that project management and construction proceed with speed and accuracy.

The passion that everyone at Droguett A&A brings to their work underscores their talent and expertise in uniting design and retail success.

Future Research Design Company (FRDC Pvt Ltd.)

#742, 8th A Main Cross, Off 80 feet road,
Koramangala 4th Block,
Bangalore-560034, India
Phone: 91-80-65391936
Fax: 91-80-41468424
Email: info@frdc.in

www.frdc.in

Addict Juice Bar

KEY PERSONNEL
Sanjay Agarwal, *Consulting and Managing Director*
Phone: +919886310645; email: sanjay@frdc.in

KEY CLIENTS
Tashi Shoes (Tata International), Ecko Unlimited (Spencer retail), Parx (Raymond), Addict (juice bar), Crusoe (mens' intimate apparel), Onida, Viveks, Nokia, ITC Ltd. (personal care division), John Players, Via (travel boutique), Eka (art store) , Max, Envy, Mr. Pretzels, Yo China, IFMPL, Fstudio (fabrics boutique), Rupee Zone (financial services), Myntra

YEAR FOUNDED
2007

NUMBER OF EMPLOYEES
24

SERVICES OFFERED
Retail Identity and concepts, Retail Design strategy, Brand Identity, Visual Merchandising, Branding, Store architectural services, Soft Experience and Service design (music, fragrance, staff attire, service brand collaterals and service wares), Green Design (LEED certified) and Roll outs so as to give a one point comprehensive solution to retailers and brand owners.

AWARDS
VMRD RETAIL DESIGN AWARDS 2009: Eka, Bangalore, India
VMRD RETAIL DESIGN AWARDS 2011:
Best Lighting Design, Tashi , Linking Store, Mumbai, India;
Best Store Front, Tashi , Linking Store, Mumbai, India

FRDC (Future Research Design Company) is a Bangalore based retail design company with exclusive licensing with internationally-reputed retail design firms ADIG Studio, San Francisco and JGA, Detroit, USA. It is a company with global vision, driven by a team of highly spirited and creative retail design professionals from India and an international team of designers and strategists. It is a consumer focused retail design company with a mission to create physical spaces which are consistent with the identity and values of the brand. It prides itself on being one of the top retail design firms in

India, providing complete 360-degree retail services, including retail concepts, design strategy, retail and brand identity, visual merchandising, branding, soft experience and service design (music, fragrance, staff attire, service brand collaterals and service wares), green design (LEED certified) and roll outs, so to provide one-point comprehensive solutions to retailers and brand owners.

The Design Approach of FRDC embraces understanding the brand values, engaging the customers, putting strategy before design, story telling, bringing concept and innovation to life, combining Indian sensibilities with international visioning and showing in every project an undying passion for details. The organization is research driven. These researches are carried out by interns from major Indian and international design institutes.

The Design Process is ever evolving and yet follows certain parameters: brand therapy (involving market surveys, research, and study of client and analysis of data), concept vision (strategic as well as space vision), profile drawings, brand design extensions and concept book manual. The multidisciplinary design team lead by qualified designers and architects from premier institutes and international experience ensures that concepts created are realistic and engineerable. FRDC works with the best professionals as associates in services such as lighting design, HVAC, structure, electrical, MEP, etc., which are incorporated into, and coordinated with, the design. FRDC strives for excellence in all specifications and details and the team demands that all vendors and suppliers adhere to acceptable and approved international/national standards.

As a member of IGBC (Indian Green Building Council) and USGBC (US Green Building Council), FRDC strives to approach design from a view of sustainability. FRDC started Green Retail design two years ago with designs for Tashi (Tata International), the first LEED certified green design stores in India. The journey has picked up pace.

FRDC is powered by a team of highly motivated and extremely creative individuals who have a vision to innovate and deliver for each client. Challenging themselves and pushing the limits of observing, learning, creating, FRDC strives fearlessly for excellence; always with the aim for integrity, knowledge, passion, perfection, vision, commitment, innovation and speed in all aspects of retail design.

Carrefour Laval Food Court

Bravo Supermercado

GHA design studios

1100 avenue des Canadiens-de-Montrèal
Bureau 130
Montréal, QC, Canada H3B 2S2
Phone: 514-843-5812 ext .229
Email: dkalisky@ghadesign.com

235 E. Main Street
Suite 107
Northville, MI 48167
Phone: 248-374-2360

www.ghadesign.com

KEY PERSONNEL
Denis Gervais, *Partner*
Steve Sutton, *Partner*
Frank Di Niro, *Partner*
Nick Giammarco, *Partner*
Paola Marques, *Partmer*
Julie Dugas, *Associate*

KEY CLIENTS:
Aéropostale, Pusateri's, H&M, Teenflo (Judith & Charles), Bravo Supermercado, Richtree

YEAR FOUNDED
1985

AWARDS
2010 Retail Store of the Year Award sponsored by Chain Store Age for Aéropostale; 2010 RDI (Retail Design Institute) for Centura Showroom; 2009 RDI for Bravo Supermercado; 2010 ICSC (International Council of Shopping Centres) U.S. Design & Development Award for Promenade in Temecula Food Court; ICSC Canadian Shopping Centre Awards for Carrefour Laval, Studio par Rona and Pickering Town Centre; 2010 SADI (Superior Achievement in Design & Imaging) for Carrefour Laval Food Court

SERVICES OFFERED
Store design, shopping centre renovations and repositioning, master retail programming, brand strategy and development

GHA is an award winning retail design firm with an international outlook culled from its unparalleled grasp of global retail. Founded in 1985, GHA has a wealth of retail experience in building memorable retail experiences. As designers for both retailers and developers, GHA has the privileged position of knowing what each one needs to succeed, what it calls "working on both sides of the lease line." With offices in Montreal and Detroit, GHA is proud of its blend of Canadian and American perspectives it brings to the international retail forum.

Au Bon Pain

Interbrand Design Forum

7575 Paragon Road
Dayton, Ohio 45459
Phone: 937-439-4400
Fax: 937-439-4340
Email: retail@interbrand.com

*As part of Interbrand, the worlds' largest branding consultancy,
we have nearly 40 offices around the globe.*

www.interbranddesignforum.com

KEY PERSONNEL
Bruce Dybvad
CEO
bruce.dybvad@interbrand.com

Tom Custer
Executive Director, Client Services
tom.custer@interbrand.com

KEY CLIENTS
Burger King, Holiday Inn, P&G, Chase, JCPenney, Au Bon Pain, Papa John's, FedEx, Applebee's,
Michaels Stores, Pollo Campero, La-Z-Boy, H&R Block, Motorola, John Deere, Honda, Yankee Candle

SERVICES OFFERED
Brand Strategy, Shopper Sciences, Packaging, Retail Design, Digital, Documentation & Rollout

Interbrand Design Forum is in the business of creating retail solutions. In a world where actions
speak louder than words, winning retailers must engage and connect to customer emotions and be
worthy of time spent. That's complicated.

Interbrand Design Forum understands retail's growing complexity and has the tools to help
companies navigate challenging market scenarios. By bringing together a diverse range of insightful
thinkers, it delivers solutions that are rigorously analytical and highly creative.

Interbrand Design Forum knows how to imaginatively frame questions, considers multiple
perspectives and celebrates instinct and intuition. The firm helps move its clients to new places.

Mars Solutions

Carlsbad, California
Phone: 760-492-3744
Fax: 760-203-9698
Email: charles@marssolutions.com

www.marssolutions.com

Canyon Market

KEY CLIENTS

Capella Hotels and Resorts , Ritz Carlton, Mandarin Oriental,
Orient–Express, Hyatt,Hilton,Marriott

SERVICES OFFERED

Retail Consulting specializing in Hospitality Industry
Store Concept Development and Design
Merchandise Analytics
Buying and Product development
Staff Selection and training
Store merchandising and Display

Mars Solutions is a retail consulting company started in 1995 with a
focus on the hospitality industry and helping clients realize retail
potential in resort, hotel and spa operations.

Directed by a senior retail executive with department and specialty
store background who utilizes extensive retail experience to help clients
develop retail concepts and execute store operational improvements.
Mars Solutions' specialties include teaching and training management
and store teams in state of art retail branding concepts, better inventory
management, sourcing and product development with a focus on a
selling and service culture in luxury store environment.

DUCE

Michael Malone Architects, Inc.

5646 Milton Street, Suite 705
Dallas, Texas 75206
Phone: 214-969-5440
Email: mmalone@mma2000.com

www.mma2000.com

KEY PERSONNEL
Michael Malone, AIA
Founding Principal
mmalone@mma2000.com

Paul J. Pascarelli, AIA, LEED AP
Principal
ppascarelli@mma2000.com

Audrey L. Maxwell, Associate AIA
Senior Designer
Audrey@mma2000.com

KEY CLIENTS
Highland Capital Management, Lockheed Martin, EDS, Shell Oil
Company, Texas New Mexico Power Company, Precision Time,
Raleigh. Ltd., Pockets Menswear, M. Penner, Harley's, Bridgettes,
Keepers, Hutson Clothing Company, The Shoe Closet

NEW CLIENT CONTACT
Michael Malone, AIA

YEAR FOUNDED
1992

NUMBER OF EMPLOYEES
Six

AWARDS
AWI Honor Award 2009 Best Commercial Project for M. Penner
2001 CEDA Award for Nautilus Theater
2000 CRSI Design Award for 2800 Lexington
2000 Metal Architecture Award for 2800 Lexington
AWI Honor Award 1993 Best Commercial Project for Melvin's Menswear
AWI Honor Award 1993 Best Commercial Project for Melvin's Children's

SERVICES OFFERED
Architecture, Interior Design, Retail Store Design and Planning

Michael Malone Architects, Inc. (MMA) is a full service architectural
firm specializing in retail store design and planning, with
additional focus in the design of single and multi-family housing,
corporate marketing centers and commercial interiors. Founded
in 1992, the award winning firm has a design oriented approach to
each project and had created unique environments for all of its
clients. For its retail projects MMA creates prototypes and
develops them as three dimensional manifestations of their clients
business culture and value proposition. Of particular interest to
the firm and a focus of a great deal of our design work is the
design of fixtures and millwork. This also has a significant impact
on our approach to residential and commercial design where built
in cabinets, paneling and custom furniture are an important
expression in all of our projects.

PDT International

2495 East Commercial Blvd
Fort Lauderdale, Florida 33308
Phone: 954-533-7240
Fax: 954-616-8434
Email: info@pdtintl.com

www.pdtintl.com

Chedraui-Tepic

KEY PERSONNEL

Sven Pavlik, *Partner,* sven@pdtintl.com
Luis Martin, *Partner,* lmartin@pdtintl.com

NUMBER OF EMPLOYEES

35

SERVICES OFFERED

Planning, Design, Project Implementation, Graphic Design

PDT International is a full service design firm, providing innovative ideas and design strategies to leading corporations around the world.

The firm's specialty lies in the customer "experience" and using that experience to develop market-driven designs maximized for performance and profitability. As a company, PDT International is committed to redefining the way people live, play, work, and shop. PDT International's strengths go far beyond pure design solutions; it is the firm's ability to create strategies that serve specific objectives that set it apart from the rest. PDT International's award-winning design team has developed successful Brand Strategies, Flagship Stores, Prototypical Retail Stores, Design Enhancements, Shop Concepts, Store-Within-A-Store and Category Management Programs for many clients since its inception.

PHILOSOPHY

PDT International's brand starts with passion; the firm is unified under the same vision and values. PDT International stands for: creativity in all it does, global in its culture and demographics, innovative in its approach, unique, spirited and bold. The team is a consumer focused group that works in collaboration to create solutions that get results and add value to the team, the consumer, the client and the industry.

APPROACH

Initially, PDT International's strategic assessment involves information gathering for it to develop a depth of understanding of where a client is today, and its future goals. The next task includes determining and verifying the key sensory elements and the emotion of the client's business, which will enable PDT International to determine the "feel". Using information learned from the assessment, goals and emotions, PDT International develops a design concept which provides the framework for further client collaboration and "Team" interaction that refines this concept to a final design. This final concept is then transformed by PDT International's production team into workable details and drawings for project implementation.

PDT International's approach is holistic – from the first forecasting and planning exercise to the creation of a new prototype — the firm is deeply involved in all components of each project. As specialist in brand creation, interpretation and implementation, PDT International captures and articulates its clients' needs today and in the future and creates the tools that are necessary to consistently embody that at every point of customer contact.

PNC Diamond Club

Perkowitz+Ruth Architects

Corporate Office
111 West Ocean Boulevard, 21st Floor
Long Beach, California 90802
Phone: 562-628-8000
Fax: 562-628-8005
Email: nmazer@prarchitects.com

Washington D.C. Office
11911 Freedom Drive, Suite 1120
Reston, Virginia 20190
Phone: 703-668-0086
Fax: 703-668-0085

www.prarchitects.com

KEY PERSONNEL

Simon Perkowitz, AIA, PE, *Founder*
Steven J. Ruth, AIA, LEED® AP, *Founder*
Branko Prebanda, *Senior Principal*
Alan Pullman, AIA, *Senior Principal*
Marios Savopoulos, *Senior Principal*
Brian E. Wolfe, AIA, *Senior Principal*
Joseph Serruya, *Associate Principal, Director of Eastern Region*

AWARDS

Gold Nugget Grand Awards;
Westside Urban Forum Design Awards;
CNU Charter Awards;
Los Angeles Conservancy President's Awards;
Long Beach Heritage Awards;
Los Angeles Business Council Awards;
SAGE Awards;
AIA National Housing Awards;
Southern California Development Forum Design Awards;
ICSC Design and Development Awards;
Superior Achievement in Design and Imaging Awards;
CMACN/AIACC Concrete Masonry Awards;
AIA Long Beach/South Bay Chapter Honor Awards;
Compass Blueprint Excellence Awards;
American Planning Association Awards;
McGraw Hill Construction Best of Awards;
NAIOP Spotlight Awards

SERVICES OFFERED

Full Scope Architectural Services; Sustainable Design,
LEED® Certification Support; Landscape Architecture;
and Forensic Architecture

Founded in 1979, Perkowitz+Ruth Architects (P+R) is a full-service architectural firm also offering landscape architecture and sustainable design services.

As a recognized leader in the field of commercial architecture, P+R's teams offer specialized expertise in retail, entertainment, hospitality and mixed-use environments. P+R understands how to create environments which are attractive to guests, residents and retailers alike. Each project is a collaborative effort. Working closely with its clients the firm seeks to discover a project's full potential through creative design, effective communication and positive working relationships.

Headquartered in California, the P+R features six offices across the United States and China, including Long Beach, CA; Portland, OR; Phoenix, AZ; Rogers, AR; Washington, DC; and Shanghai. Agile, focused studios provide clients with the benefit of personal service and targeted expertise. The firm's inter-office collaborative approach allows it the ability to apply resources as necessary to meet the varying requirements of every project.

P+R's staff of 200-plus professionals consists of licensed architects, landscape designers and United States Green Building Council LEED®-accredited professionals. The firm is licensed to practice in all 50 states and is an official ENERGY STAR Service Provider. As members of the Urban Land Institute, International Council of Shopping Centers and American Institute of Architects, among other notable local and national organizations, P+R is active in the industry and within each of its local communities.

Giacomo

plajer & franz studio

Erkelenzdamm 59-61
10999 Berlin, Germany
Phone: +49 30 616 558 0
Email: studio@plajer-franz.de

www.plajer-franz.de

KEY PERSONNEL

Alexander Plajer, *Principal*
Werner Franz, *Principal*

NUMBER OF EMPLOYEES

45

KEY CLIENTS

BMW Group, PUMA, Timberland Europe, s.Oliver, Samsung, Galeries Lafayette, Adessa, Estée Lauder, Salewa

SERVICES OFFERED

Architecture, Interior Architecture, Consultancy, Conceptual Design, Design and Planning, Graphic Design

The company founders, architects alexander plajer & werner franz, gained their initial international experience in New York at the office of Richard Meier and Tsao & McKown. Here they both spent several years working with clients in the United States and the middle and far east before moving back to Germany to set up their own company in Berlin in 1996. In over a decade of creative and imaginative partnership, they built up an impressively broad-ranging portfolio with an international client base. Today plajer & franz studio with their team of 45 employees has an international reputation for innovative excellence and a superb sense of style. Their projects are regularly featured in publications worldwide.

The development of brand architecture and corporate identity in retail as well as the design of premium hotels and resorts form the core of the firm's expertise. plajer & franz studio has an international reputation for innovative excellence,

quality down to the smallest detail, great planning skills and a superb sense of style.

From private yacht to automobile trade stands via award-winning bars and luxury hotels, the key to plajer & franz studio's freshness of vision lies in their continuous exploration and cross-fertilisation between disciplines and areas of experience. The firm's ability to deliver show-stoppingly innovative design with elegant and meticulous finishing and precise details lies with its ability to take what they learn in one area and applying it, where appropriate, in another: high tech material forming from the car industry, for example, may yield exciting new surfaces for a shop-in-shop project, whereas new developments in the use of digital display techniques from the bar and club scene might fit perfectly with a new automobile display concept – it 's all in the mix!

At plajer & franz studio all project stages, from concept to design as well as roll-out supervision, are carried out in-house by plajer & franz' hand-picked team of 45 architects, interior and graphic designers. Special project-based groups work on overall interior and building construction projects and on communication and graphic design. plajer & franz studio have also established themselves in the premium sector of luxury residential projects and hotels in both Europe and Asia; these include a recently completed hotel in Porto, a five star resort in Croatia and 50,000 m2 premium serviced apartments on the Portuguese coast.

Café Mixup

Plus Construction Group

Prol. Av. De los bosques 1506 piso 2 c.p.52780
Tecamachalco, Estado de México
Phone: 52451096 – 52451291 - 52451589
Fax: 52451589 Ext.237
Email: t.plusart@gmail.com

www.cplus.com.mx

NEW CLIENT CONTACT
Lic. Tadeo Carreño Cole, email: t.plusart@gmail.com

AWARDS
International Design Awards, Honorable Mention, Vespa

Over the course of its 45-year history, Plus Construction Group has successfully designed and built a multitude of industrial, commercial and residential projects. Clients such as Modelo Brewery, the music-store chain Mix-up and entertainment companies iShop and Apple have all benefited from the firm's high standards in customer service, quality of design, workmanship, and professionalism.

Plus Construction Group's experienced team of architects and engineers are always available and willing to face new challenges and partner with their clients to produce the best possible results for each project. As they reinvent and redefine the aesthetic principles of design – pushing the boundaries and taking risks when needed or respecting conservative standards when appropriate — each employee contributes to the firm's continued development both in Mexico and internationally.

Ole'

blt* supermarket

rkd retail/iQ

gpf witthayu towers suite 703-704 tower A
93/1 wireless road
bangkok 10330 thailand
Phone: +66225531550
Email: talk2us@rkdretailiq.com

shanghai / shenzhen / hong kong / mumbai / dubai

www.rkdretailiq.com

KEY PERSONNEL

RKurt Durrant, *president & idea man*
email: rkurt@rkdretailiq.com

KEY CLIENTS

DFS Galleria, China Resources, Suning, Parkson

NEW CLIENT CONTACT

RKurt Durrant

YEAR FOUNDED

1987

NUMBER OF EMPLOYEES

50+

AWARDS

To date 11 projects have been recognized by a variety of
leading international retail industry organizations yielding
22 awards for retail planning and design excellence.

rkd retail/iQ is full service retail design consultancy specialized in
delivering complete branded retail environments across all retail
formats and channels.

Retail planning + design / retail + environmental graphics / retail
architecture / retail strategy.

Through its convergent process of retail strategy and retail
planning + design, rkd retail/iQ partners with clients who share a
common vision of positioning their retail brand in the competitive
world market.

Celebrating 24 years of specific Asian retail planning and design
experience in 2011, rkd retail/iQ has completed hundreds of retail
projects with dozens of clients resulting in millions of square meters
of implemented retail and multiple awards.

rkd retail/iQ has directed/participated/completed retail projects in
20 countries and developed programs that have been implemented
in a further 15 countries.

Through organic expansion rkd retail/iQ has evolved into 6 group
offices in China (Shanghai, Shenzhen, Hong Kong), India (Mumbai),
MENA (Dubai) with the group head quarters in Thailand (Bangkok).
rkd retail/iQ currently staffed by 50+ retail design team members
from an exciting and diverse variety of experiences and cultures.

La Provence Artisanal French Bakery & Café

Ruscio Studio

2197 Sherbrooke E.
Montréal, Québec, Canada H2K 1C8
Phone: 514-276-0600
Fax: 514-276-6604
Email: info@rusciostudio.com

www.rusciostudio.com

KEY CLIENTS
Starbucks

AWARDS
Floor Focus 2011 Vision Awards
Retail category winner
Project: Magico Imperial

Chain Store Age Awards 2010
Honorable Mention - Soft Line Category
Project: Verona Vibe

A.R.E. Design Awards 2010
Fixture of the Year
Project: Mark's Walk-in Freezer Lab

VMSD 2010 Retail Renovation Competition
Renovation of the Year
Project: Underground

GIA World 2010
Global Innovator Award
Project: Stark & Whyte

SERVICES OFFERED
Concept development
Brand development
Project management
Mall renovation / expansion
Tenant reviews
Site surveys
Site supervision & coordination
Permit expediting

ROBERT RUSCIO BIOGRAPHY
President/Principal Designer
President and Principal Designer of Ruscio Studio, Robert Ruscio is a 25 year veteran in the retail design industry and is widely recognized in the field for his passion and talent in the conceptualization of retail spaces.

Having gained valuable experience in various commercial design firms where he worked as team leader on "roll-out" projects such as Timberland, Aldo, Pegabo, Les Ailes de la Mode, San Francisco, Dynamite, Stokes, etc., Robert stepped out on his own and created Ruscio Studio in 2002.

RUSCIO STUDIO
Now in its 10th year, Ruscio Studio has grown into an interior retail design firm that is recognized, both nationally and internationally, by retailers and malls alike.

With a reputation for a current and fresh approach to retail concepts, it is the fusion of design expertise with wide retail knowledge that makes Ruscio Studio uniquely specialized. The firm listens to its clients and offers them complete expertise to fulfill their needs, yet never loses sight of the main purpose of its involvement — RETAIL.

Ruscio Studio is driven by the pride of its work and the ability to "turn on a dime". Understanding deadlines and being challenged is what the firm has come to expect. The team holds over 100 years of combined experience directly in the field and is ready to deliver to its clients.

Ruscio Studio has been honored with over 70 local and international awards from respected organizations such as ARE, ICSC, VMSD and SADI.

Whole Foods Market

Studio One Eleven

111 West Ocean Boulevard, 20th Floor
Long Beach, California 90802
Phone: 562-901-1500
Fax: 562-901-1501
Email: nmazer@studio-111.com

www.studio-111.com

KEY PERSONNEL

Alan Pullman, AIA, *Senior Principal*
Michael Bohn, AIA, *Principal*
Winston Chang, AIA, LEED® AP, *Principal*

AWARDS

Gold Nugget Grand Awards;
Westside Urban Forum Design Awards;
CNU Charter Awards;
Los Angeles Conservancy President's Awards;
Long Beach Heritage Awards;
Los Angeles Business Council Awards;
SAGE Awards;
AIA National Housing Awards;
Southern California Development Forum Design Awards;
ICSC Design and Development Awards;
Superior Achievement in Design and Imaging Awards;
CMACN/AIACC Concrete Masonry Awards;
AIA Long Beach/South Bay Chapter Honor Awards;
Compass Blueprint Excellence Awards;
American Planning Association Awards;
McGraw Hill Construction Best of Awards;
NAIOP Spotlight Awards

SERVICES OFFERED

Full Scope Architectural Services; Sustainable Design,
LEED® Certification Support; and Landscape Architecture

Studio One Eleven is a distinct division of Perkowitz+Ruth Architects dedicated to creating more vibrant communities through an integrated practice of architecture, landscape and urban design. From urban strategies operating at scales ranging from the block to the city, to architectural projects located on urban infill sites, rigorous design criteria informs all of our work.

Studio One Eleven believes that the purpose of architecture is the making of more livable and sustainable cities. From the geography of the region to the layout of blocks and buildings, every urban component has an interdependent relationship with all others. The firm views each project as an opportunity to physically enhance the urban context that it sustains.

While committed to architectural solutions that represent contemporary buildings of its time, Studio One Eleven designs are not predicated by a singular language but are inspired through the careful assessment of the place where they stand. The firm believes that the best way to enhance or create the future of a place is to respect and understand its past patterns and precedents.

With 40% of its staff LEED® accredited, designing for the lowest possible impact on the environment is the foundation for all of Studio One Eleven's work. Sustainability is integral to the firm's creative process and the team designs to the highest degree preferred by its clients. Studio One Eleven has completed or are designing several new developments to meet LEED Silver requirements, including a new preschool and several large mixed use developments. In addition, Studio One Eleven has completed an office complex that is the first to follow the City of Long Beach's Green Building Policy and was done on a voluntary basis.

Ben & Jerry's

Tesser Inc

121 2nd Street, Floor 7
San Francisco, California 94105
Phone: 415-541-9999
Fax: 415-541-9699
Email: tre.musco@tesser.com

www.tesser.com

KEY PERSONNEL

Tré Musco, *CEO and Chief Creative Officer*

KEY CLIENTS

Chili's, Wendy's, Ben & Jerry's, Denny's, Del Taco, Baja Fresh, IHOP, Quiznos, Cost Plus World Market

NEW CLIENT CONTACT

Tre Musco

YEAR FOUNDED

1993

NUMBER OF EMPLOYEES

10-15

AWARDS

Several (QSR Packaging, gold award, 2 years in a row)

SERVICES OFFERED

Comprehensive brand strategy and consumer insights work, corporate identity, retail (store) design – 3D, 2 graphic design for a number of touch points including print, packaging, uniforms, merchandising programs, menu board expertise

Since 1993, Tesser has been building powerful brands by focusing on the big picture: 360 degrees of uncompromised thinking on branding and integrated design. As strategic consultants, designers, and branding experts, Tesser helps clients create both long-term brand value and highly effective design programs. Tesser provides a unique mix of strategy, naming and verbal branding, corporate identity, retail design, merchandising, packaging design, and website design.

Based in San Francisco, Tesser's clients include Denny's, KFC, Ben & Jerry's, Chili's, Del Taco, Williamson-Dickie (makers of Dickies workwear), Musco Family Olive Co., Popeyes and Baja Fresh.

TPG Architecture

360 Park Avenue South
New York, New York 10010
Phone: 212-768-0800
www.tpgarchitecture.com

La Birreria

KEY PERSONNEL

James G. Phillips, AIA, *Founder*
Frederic Strauss, AIA, *Principal*
James T. Doherty, AIA, *Principal*
Michel Fiechter, *Principal*
Michael Hayes, AIA, LEED AP, *Principal*
Michael Brandt, AIA, *Principal*
William Alisse, AIA, *Principal*
Alec Zaballero, *Principal*
Pamela Jacobs, LEED AP, *Director of Marketing*

YEAR FOUNDED

1979

NUMBER OF EMPLOYEES

150

TPG Architecture (TPG) was founded in 1979 in New York City, and has remained headquartered here throughout its 32 year history. The firm is a leader in the field of architecture and interior design and has performed services for a wide range of market sectors, designing and managing projects throughout the region, the nation, and overseas. TPG has grown from its initial dual partnership to a practice with approximately 150 professionals in three offices. In addition to its headquarters, TPG has offices in Long Island and London.

TPG services numerous market sectors including: advertising, broadcasting (advanced technology), corporate, education, entertainment, finance, government, healthcare, hospitality, insurance, legal, non-profit, pharmaceutical, publishing, residential and retail.

Longo's

Watt International Inc.

300 Bayview Avenue
Toronto, Ontario, M5A 3R7
Phone: 416-364-9384
Fax: 416-364-1098
Email: contactus@wattisretail.com

China Office:
24F,520 YiShan Road
Shanghai 200235
P.R. China

www.wattisretail.com

KEY PERSONNEL
Patrick Rodmell, *President and CEO*
Glen Kerr, *EVP Creative and Client Services*

YEAR FOUNDED
1966

NUMBER OF EMPLOYEES
60

NEW CLIENT CONTACT
Email: contactus@wattisretail.com

AWARDS
Longo's has won 4 awards. Watt International
has won 12 awards in the past year for retail design
and packagaing.

SERVICES OFFERED

Research (consumer and shopper research, financial analysis, stakeholder interviews, trends and innovation reports, SWOT and best practice analysis, Need state and path to purchase modeling)

Strategy (brand positioning, marketing strategies, channel strategies, product and merchandise strategies, private brand architecture, business and strategic planning, management consulting, performance measurement (KPIs)

Creative (brand name, identity and guidelines, retail design, package design, merchandising and POP displays, integrated communications, brandvertising, web, mobile and social media, total production management, value engineering)

Watt International is a truly integrated retail agency, with over forty years experience in over forty countries around the world. Working collaboratively with its clients, Watt International helps uncover the most meaningful insights, set the right strategies, and deliver results-oriented creative solutions across every brand touchpoint.

MARKETING-JAZZ, 188
Huelva 16, Bloque 2, Estudio 54
28100 Alcobendas, Madrid, Spain
Phone: +34 91 484 02 30
Email: info@marketing-jazz.com
www.marketing-jazz.com

Mars Solutions, 144
Carlsbad, California
Phone: 760-492-3744
Email: charles@marssolutions.com
www.marssolutions.com

Michael Malone Architects, Inc., 40
5646 Milton Street, Suite 705
Dallas, Texas 75206
Phone: 214-969-5440
Email: mmalone@mma2000.com
www.mma2000.com

PDT International, 94
2495 East Commercial Blvd
Fort Lauderdale, Florida 33308
Phone: 954-533-7240
Email: info@pdtintl.com
www.pdtintl.com

Perennial Inc., 174
15 Waulron Street
Toronto, Ontario, M9C 1B4 Canada
Phone: 877-617-8315
www.perennialinc.com

Perkowitz+Ruth Architects, 68
111 West Ocean Boulevard, 21st Floor
Long Beach, California 90802
Phone: 562-628-8000
Email: nmazer@prarchitects.com
www.prarchitects.com

plajer & franz studio, 46
Erkelenzdamm 59-61
10999 Berlin, Germany
Phone: +49 30 616 558 0
Email: studio@plajer-franz.de
www.plajer-franz.de

Plus Construction Group, 30
Prol. Av. De los bosques 1506 piso 2 c.p.52780
Tecamachalco, Estado de México
Phone: 52451096 – 52451291 - 52451589
Email: t.plusart@gmail.com
www.cplus.com.mx

rkd retail/iQ, 84, 122
gpf witthayu towers suite 703-704 tower A
93/1 wireless road, bangkok 10330 thailand
Phone: +66225531550
Email: talk2us@rkdretailiq.com
www.rkdretailiq.com

Ruscio Studio, 58
2197 Sherbrooke E.
Montréal, Québec, Canada H2K 1C8
Phone: 514-276-0600
Email: info@rusciostudio.com
www.rusciostudio.com

Store Design Services, 88
6533 Flying Cloud Drive Suite 100
Minneapolis, Minnesota 55344-3307
Phone: 877-374-8258
www.storedesignservices.com

Studio One Eleven, 134
111 West Ocean Boulevard, 20th Floor
Long Beach, California 90802
Phone: 562-901-1500
Email: nmazer@studio-111.com
www.studio-111.com

Tesser Inc. 24
121 2nd Street, Floor 7
San Francisco, California 94105
Phone: 415-541-9999
Email: tre.musco@tesser.com
www.tesser.com

TPG Architecture, 54, 156
360 Park Avenue South,
New York, New York 10010
Phone: 212-768-0800
www.tpgarchitecture.com

Tricario Architecture & Design, 184
502 Valley Road
Wayne, New Jersey 07470
Phone: 973-692-0222
Email: info@tricario.com
www.tricario.com

Watt International Inc., 108
300 Bayview Avenue
Toronto, Ontario, M5A 3R7
Phone: 416-364-9384
Email: contactus@wattisretail.com
www.wattisretail.com